THE ROLE OF RELIGIOUS ORGANIZATIONS IN SOCIAL MOVEMENTS

THE ROLE OF RELIGIOUS ORGANIZATIONS IN SOCIAL MOVEMENTS

Edited by
BARBARA M. YARNOLD

PRAEGER

New York
Westport, Connecticut
London

Library of Congress Cataloging-in-Publication Data

The Role of religious organizations in social movements / edited by
    Barbara M. Yarnold.
        p.   cm.
    Includes bibliographical references and index.
    ISBN 0–275–94017–9 (alk. paper)
    1. United States—Religious and ecclesiastical institutions.
    2. Social movements—United States.   I. Yarnold, Barbara M., 1961– .
    BL2525.R64   1991
    306.6′9165′0973—dc20   91–7206

British Library Cataloguing in Publication Data is available.

Library of Congress Catalog Card Number: 91–7206
ISBN: 0–275–94017–9

First published in 1991

Praeger Publishers, One Madison Avenue, New York, NY 10010
An imprint of Greenwood Publishing Group, Inc.

Printed in the United States of America

The paper used in this book complies with the
Permanent Paper Standard issued by the National
Information Standards Organization (Z39.48-1984).

10 9 8 7 6 5 4 3 2 1

Copyright Acknowledgments

The author and publisher are grateful to the following for allowing the use
of material:

Material in Chapter 2 originally appeared in Andrew S. McFarland, "Public
Interest Lobbies Versus Minority Faction" in Allan J. Cigler and Budett A.
Loomis, *Interest Group Politics* (Washington, D.C.: Congressional Quarterly
Press, 1983), 324–53.

R. Golden and M. McConnell, *Sanctuary: The New Underground Railroad*
(New York: Orbis Books, 1986).

To the meek and the caretakers

Contents

Preface

This volume examines the role of religious organizations in U.S. social movements. Starting from the theoretical base of J. Freeman and Andrew S. McFarland (Chapter 2), which posits that interest groups often provide important communications networks which facilitate the spread of core ideas of social movements, the volume examines the extent to which religious organizations have helped to spread U.S. social movements, including the sanctuary movement, the gay and lesbian rights movement, the peace movement, and the fundamentalist Christian movement. I suggest in Chapter 3 that social movements arise when a collective decision is made to follow the natural law over the positive law when the two conflict. Further, religious organizations are likely participants in social movements since they are generally committed to natural law precepts. Hence, religious organizations may become involved in social movements and act as the important communications system for a social movement's ideas, when the ideas of the social movement are consistent with the religious tenets of the religion in question. Hence, for example, religious organizations played an important role in spreading the core ideas of the sanctuary movement (Chapter 3), peace movement (Chapter 4), and fundamentalist Christian movement (Chapter 6). However, the gay and lesbian rights movement (Chapter 5) was not communicated by major religious organizations in the U.S. since they were opposed to gay and lesbian lifestyles. Gay and lesbian rights organizations responded to this lack of religious support by creating their own religious organizations which, after their formation, did play a role in communicating this movement.

The fact that religious organizations perform the task of communicating the core ideas of social movements contributes to movement success in two important respects. First, religious organizations have inherent legitimacy that may help legitimize the movement. Second, if the social movement is heavily dependent upon religious organizations, it may have a longer life span than most social movements which tend to dissipate as public attention to the issues diminishes and funds to movement organizations become depleted. Since religious organizations have a constant source of organizational support (from their congregations), a social movement which is church-based (such as the sanctuary movement) may have a longer life span than other social movements, losing momentum not due to a lack of public support, but due to a loss of interest on the part of religious leaders.

Acknowledgments

I would like to sincerely thank those who made this work possible, including those teachers who, throughout all of my educational endeavors, were dedicated to knowledge and, more importantly, independent thinking. Most recently, in a Ph.D. program at the University of Illinois at Chicago, I was fortunate to run into two inspiring political science scholars, Professors Andrew S. McFarland and Lettie M. Wenner. Credit is due to Pauline Broderick, my graduate assistant, for preparing the Index with great effort and precision.

At great personal cost, my family members provided the love, intellectual environment, and emotional and financial support necessary for the long course of work in which I have been engaged. I remember our many family discussions, heated debates, soul-searching late evenings of cigarettes and coffee, shared. I must thank them all, including my mother, Helen Maria Yarnold; Irena Maria Suszko, my aunt and dear friend; my dear sister, Suzan Maria Yarnold; and my brothers, Paul Richard Yarnold, Ph.D., Charles Nicholas Yarnold, James Alexander Yarnold, and Jack Christopher Yarnold.

Also, I dedicate this to the memory of my deceased father, James Knapps Yarnold, Ph.D., and to my deceased grandparents, especially Stanislawa and Micolaj Suszko.

THE ROLE OF RELIGIOUS ORGANIZATIONS IN SOCIAL MOVEMENTS

Chapter 1

Introduction

Barbara M. Yarnold

This volume focuses upon the role played by religious organizations in various social movements that have arisen in the United States. The social movements which are examined include the sanctuary movement, the peace movement between the wars, the gay and lesbian rights movement, and the evangelical movement.

Two major questions are addressed. The first is what caused these religious organizations to become involved in the social movement in question. The second relates to what are the likely implications of this involvement of religious organizations in social movements.

In Chapter 2, "Public Interest Lobbies Versus Minority Faction," Andrew S. McFarland posits that the involvement of religious organizations in social movements facilitates the spread of the core ideas of the movement to the general public and policymakers, including political entrepreneurs. The reason that religious organizations are so effective in performing this role is that they have an established communications system with which to communicate with members of their congregations, who become "captive audiences" for their ideas. McFarland points to the important role played by black Protestant churches in communicating the core ideas of the civil rights movement to the U.S. public and, eventually, to policymakers in the United States.

Another important point, derived from Freeman's work in 1975, that McFarland addresses is the concept that new, pro-movement interest groups are often formed during the course of a social movement. These groups may continue to exist even after the social movement has waned, thus providing a source of countervailing power to interest groups.

In Chapter 3, "The Role of Religious Organizations in the U.S. Sanctuary Movement," my analysis supports both of McFarland's theories: religious organizations were not only important in communicating the core ideas of the sanctuary movement which arose in the early 1980s, but theirs was virtually the only voice of the movement. The sanctuary movement also spawned the formation of new, pro-movement groups which provided a source of countervailing power. These groups provided services to refugees which ranged from advocacy to giving Central American refugees sanctuary.

I add that the involvement of religious organizations in the U.S. sanctuary movement had two other significant effects. First, in accordance with McFarland's analysis, the ideas of the sanctuary movement were legitimized through their adoption by religious organizations. Second, the sanctuary movement has a greater likelihood of enduring than most social movements since it is a movement that is almost entirely sustained by religious organizations. Religious organizations have a constant source of support from their congregations, and need not make public appeals for support to the same extent as the leaders of other social movements, such as the environmental protection movement. Hence, if the sanctuary movement wanes, this will be due more to a loss of interest on the part of religious leaders than due to a lack of resources.

I extend my analysis to the question of what caused religious organizations to become involved in the U.S. sanctuary movement. In attempting to explain this involvement, I posit that there are two general categories of interest groups in the United States: "entrenched" organizations and "fringe" organizations. The distinction between the two is that "entrenched" organizations tend to be committed to the positive law and preserving the status quo, since they rely for their support upon other "entrenched" interests such as corporations and government. "Fringe" organizations, in contrast, are primarily committed to natural law precepts, and do not rely for their support upon "entrenched" interests.

I argue that fringe organizations are the most likely participants in social movements, and are often the only voice for the main ideas of a social movement. Entrenched organizations are less likely to become involved in social movements since this may jeopardize their financial support.

In the context of the U.S. sanctuary movement, the religious organizations which both initiated and perpetuated the movement were "fringe" organizations. The positive law in the United States (U.S. immigration laws and their adjudicative interpretations) failed to provide Central Americans with refuge in the United States; though Central American refugees were entitled to apply for political asylum, refugee status, and withholding of deportation, their applications for relief were overwhelmingly denied. This conflicted with a natural law precept, long respected in Judeo-Christian practices, of granting refuge to those who are homeless or fear persecution in their homes.

I suggest that social movements, including the U.S. sanctuary movement, arise when a collective decision is made to follow the natural law over the positive law when the two conflict. Further, I anticipate that religious organizations will generally play an important role in social movements due to their historical commitment to natural law unless, of course, the core ideas of social movements conflict with the dogma of religious organizations.

In Chapter 4, "The Role of Religious Organizations in the Peace Movement Between the Wars," William R. Marty discusses the peace movement which emerged in the United States and Great Britain during the period between World War I and World War II. The peace movement was initiated by Protestant religious organizations, which actively communicated the core ideas of the movement to the public and policymakers. These core ideas rejected the validity of war under any circumstances, and any policy which might trigger war. Hence, leaders of the peace movement rejected the positive laws of the United States and Great Britain insofar as they promoted war or increased the likelihood of war.

According to Marty, the interwar peace movement was quite successful in gaining organizational support: "The spread of pacifism among the churches and within religious organizations between the World Wars was both rapid and extensive."

The peace movement mobilized sufficient countervailing power to defeat, at least temporarily, powerful military-industrial complexes which existed in both the U.S. and Great Britain, which tend to lobby in favor of increased armaments. Unlike the sanctuary movement, Marty claims that the peace movement enjoyed great policy success in both the United States and Great Britain, which went into World War II unprepared for war after having offered no defense of their allies.

Marty also engages in a fascinating discussion of the "hybrid" or "new" pacifism which was at the base of the inter-war peace movement, and the inherent fallacies of the new pacifism. Specifically, Marty asserts that Christian religious organizations have operated within three traditions on questions of war and peace: pacifism, just war theory, and the crusade. Traditional pacifism was characterized by a withdrawal from the world; traditional just war theory and the crusade by engagement in the world.

In the period between World Wars I and II, the new pacifism which developed was a pacifism that was politically engaged in the world. Marty suggests that the new, politically engaged pacifism was made ineffective in the world by its pacifist commitment. He adds that this failure explains both why traditional pacifism withdrew from the world and why Christians who assume political responsibility develop just war theories.

In Chapter 5, Steven H. Haeberle examines "The Role of Religious Organizations in the Gay and Lesbian Rights Movement." Haeberle's analysis reveals that religious organizations do not actively participate in all social movements. In fact, some religious organizations obstructed efforts of those engaged in the gay and lesbian rights movement. As a general proposition, a religious organization will not become involved in a social movement when the core ideas of the social movement are inconsistent with the tenets of the religion in question.

The opposition of religious organizations to the gay and lesbian rights movement is not altogether surprising when one considers that legal prohibitions on homosexual activity have been based largely on religious dogma. Hence, the core ideas of the gay and lesbian rights movement have not, for the most part, been communicated by major religious organizations in the United States since they are opposed to gay and lesbian lifestyles.

There are some exceptions, however. Haeberle claims that religious groups with a humanistic world view will be the first to adopt revised theological arrangements (such as gay and lesbian clergy and same-sex marriages), while those religious organizations which insist on the preservation of a more rigid dogma will resist such modifications. Hence, the gay and lesbian rights movement was more readily received by groups such as the Unitarians and the Quakers, which are committed to social justice, while the movement has had little success in fundamentalist sects such as the Evangelicals and Pentecostals.

Acceptance of the core ideas of the gay and lesbian rights movement by the Quakers and the Unitarians was significant for a few reasons. First, religious leaders within these organizations communicated the core ideas of the movement—nondiscrimination against gays and lesbians—to their congregations and, to some extent, the general public. Another important result is that the movement was legitimized through its association with established religious organizations. Further, countervailing power grew not only externally, as gay rights organizations increased throughout American society, but also internally, as gay and lesbian rights organizations formed within established religious organizations.

Most religious organizations, however, failed to take any type of role in the gay and lesbian rights movement. Gay and lesbian rights advocates responded to this lack of religious support by creating their own religious organizations which, after their formation, did play some role in communicating the core ideas of the movement. Examples include the Universal Fellowship of the Metropolitan Community Church (UFMCC), which is a Christian church for gays and lesbians. Since these organizations are comprised primarily of gay and lesbian members, however, the communication functions of these organizations are of limited scope. Compensating for this to some extent is that the UFMCC encourages its members to engage in social activism, and has sponsored marches, demonstrations, and sit-ins, which are often reported by the media.

In Chapter 6, Mel Hailey shifts to cultural analysis in his article on "The Role of Religious Organizations in Evangelical Political Activity: The Moral Majority and Evangelicals for Social Action." This insightful analysis contains a warning: Those religious organizations which become too enmeshed in social movements may have their legitimacy and existence threatened when they stray too far from the essential tenets of their religions. For example, Hailey demonstrates how Evangelicals for Social Action (ESA), through its involvement in evangelical political activity in the 1970s and 1980s, made a critical departure from its early Christian origins, which were hierarchical, to egalitarianism. He wonders whether ESA, a culturally torn organization, can withstand the contradictions.

However, Hailey offers a prescription for religious organizations which seek to be involved in social movements. Perhaps the best way to avoid the contradictions faced by ESA is to adopt the strategy of Jerry Falwell. According to Hailey: "Jerry Falwell and the Moral Majority developed an ingenious way to bridge the boundary that would allow him to remain theologically pure in the competition of the marketplace." Although foremost a televangelist and pastor of a Baptist church, Falwell felt the need to become involved in American politics. To this end, in 1980 he formed a nonreligious political organization, the Moral Majority, which attracted support from many different religious denominations, uniting them around protection of the family and religious values in American politics. The Moral Majority was relatively short-lived. When the social movement had achieved some of its major policy goals, Falwell announced in June 1989 that it was being disbanded.

Chapter 2

Public Interest Lobbies Versus Minority Faction

Andrew S. McFarland

REPRESENTATIVE INTEREST GROUPS

In the 1950s, political scientist David Truman and other "group theorists" argued that the panoply of organized interests was a roughly accurate measure of the interests held by individuals. Group theorists believed that (1) people know their own interests; (2) they are able without inordinate difficulty to organize these interests into political groups; (3) American political institutions provide numerous opportunities for organized interest groups to influence the political process; (4) the resulting public policy is usually representative, because it reflects the balance of power among organized interests, whose relative strength in turn is a measure of the relative incidence of interests among individual citizens.

These assumptions constitute a large part of the "interest group liberalism" so roundly denounced by Professor Theodore Lowi. Moreover, these group theory propositions are now in disrepute, largely because of their refutation in Mancur Olson's *The Logic of Collective Action.* But group theory cannot be totally invalidated. Political groups have been organized to represent diffuse but widely shared interests such as protecting the consumer, maintaining a clean environment, and combatting corruption in government. Such groups include the "public interest groups," supported by a middle-class constituency.

SOCIAL MOVEMENTS

Social movements are another phenomenon inconsistent with the minority faction argument. By "social movement," one might denote recent political developments such as the black civil rights movement, the women's movement, environmentalism, consumerism, the peace movement of the 1960s, or the conservative activism of Christian fundamentalism and the tax revolt of 1977–1980. While the term "social movement" is widely used, it is difficult to define. For our purposes, a social movement is characterized by activity directed toward changing institutions and behaviors of importance to a society, as opposed to peripheral institutions or routine behaviors. Another defining feature of a social movement is its mode of political expression, often consisting of unconventional tactics and behaviors, such as civil disobedience, organizing demonstrations, breaking up into small groups for the purpose of "consciousness raising," and even the threat or actual use of violence.

Writers such as Grant McConnell, E. E. Schattschneider, and Olson published their works before the impact of the black civil rights movement and the other movements of the 1960s. Writing later, Lowi ascribed some political importance to social movements, but stressed their imminent bureaucratization, increasing control by organizational oligarchies, and acceptance of the status quo. Nonetheless, social movements are sometimes an important part of American politics and have been associated with major public policy changes such as federal initiation of civil rights laws and federal regulation of pollution.

THE CHARACTERISTICS OF
SOCIAL MOVEMENTS

Intuitively, it seems that the impact of the black civil rights movement, the women's movement, and the various public interest movements (environmentalism, consumerism, government reform) have been quite significant in changing American society and politics since the 1950s. Moreover, social movements have an additional analytical significance—they are a source of countervailing power to "special interest" groups.

Recent social movements in America can be categorized in Madisonian terms. One type of movement is that of some minority—such as blacks, Native Americans, or homosexuals—that protests what is seen to be a majority faction, a majority "united and actuated by some common impulse of passion, or of interest, adverse to the rights of other citizens." A second type of social movement protests what are considered to be instances of minority faction, in which a minority "actuated by some common . . . interest, adverse to the rights of other citizens" acts adversely "to the permanent and aggregate interests of the community." Often, protestors against minority tyranny have claimed to be speaking for a majority, as opposed to being just one minority protesting the actions of another.

Crusading Against The Special Interests

The Progressives of the early twentieth century (1900–1917) and the "public interest movement" that flourished in the early 1970s had much in common, both relying heavily on the rhetorical symbolism of defending public interests against special interests. Many of the leaders of both movements apparently believed in a theory of special interest dominance, similar to the minority faction argument. The Progressives, for instance, typically believed that state and local governments had been undermined by coalitions of political party bosses, government employees, and corrupt contractors stealing from the public treasury. The Progressives frequently saw members of the U.S. Congress as agents of the oil "monopoly," big Wall Street banks, the railroad industry, and so forth.

Similarly, modern public interest advocates frequently state a version of the minority faction paradigm. Leaders of the Common Cause—on the "establishment" end of the public interest movement—have on several occasions argued that American government succumbs too easily to control by special interests. Ralph Nader has emphasized the danger that corporate-bureaucratic alliances may undermine the enforcement of legislation he has supported. In the era of Interior Secretary James Watt, environmentalists articulated concern about special interest coalitions of energy corporations and the Department of the Interior scheming to exploit publicly owned land.

The values of the Progressives and of the recent public interest advocates overlapped considerably. Both movements had environmental programs, known as Conservation in the Progressive era when Gifford Pinchot and others pressed for the expansion of the national parks and the protection of American woodlands. Other Progressives foreshadowed 1970s consumerists. In their campaigns to regulate industry, Progressives passed the first federal meatpacking inspection act and actively pursued the regulation of railroads, insurance, banking, and other industries. In addition, the Progressives were extremely active in reforming the institutional mechanisms of government to combat the "special interests." The turn-of-the-century reformers introduced such measures as primary elections, the initiative and referendum, the city manager system, hiring public employees according to civil service rules, nonpartisan elections, and other measures designed to promote popular rule and "economy and efficiency in government," and to combat the purported excesses of political bosses and party hacks in government.

The Middle-Class Presence

Both the Progressive movement and the recent public interest movement were characterized by a predominance of the middle class among their supporters. These were not movements led by the wealthy or by large corporations, nor were they movements particularly favored by blue-collar workers, minorities, or the poor. Turn-of-the-century Progressives—often small-business-men, teachers, prosperous farmers, ministers, lawyers, doctors, scientists, and journalists—were ordinarily described as better educated and more prosperous than their fellow citizens. Interpretations of the middle-class nature of Progressivism differ; some writers have argued that the middle-class protestors were co-opted by large corporations or by wealthy elites at the local level. But the predominantly middle-class nature of Progressive supporters is seldom disputed.

Progressivism, the public interest movement, and the women's movement were both inside and outside of the social and political mainstream in their beginnings. New ideas about the environment, the rights of consumers, and the need for public funding of elections were unconventional, but they began to be advocated by people close to the sociological norm of the country (the white middle class), many of whom had the communications skills and political talents to influence other members of the educated middle class and to lobby political elites. In this situation, the preexisting variety of social institutions at the disposal of the middle class (universities, communications media, publishers, political party organizations, churches, professional associations, civic associations, etc.) hastened the spread of the new ideas of their social movement by providing forums for communication. At certain times in American history, middle-class social movements have appeared suddenly and have had an immediate impact on public policy, partly because existing social institutions provided a means of communicating the ideas of the new movement.

THE POLITICAL DYNAMICS OF SOCIAL MOVEMENTS IN AMERICA

Social movements may act as checks upon the power of minority faction by a variety of mechanisms, including the access to influential institutions and possession of political leverage that may result from a movement's deep roots in society. Following are a number of the forces that contribute to the success or failure of social movements.

Intermediary Groups

Political movements usually form coalitions with some established interest groups, elements of political parties, and individual political candidates. Such intermediary groups and politicians legitimate some of the new ideas of the movement and spread such ideas through preexisting communications networks. Intermediary groups also provide an organizational basis for lobbying Congress, the federal executive branch, and state governments. In addition, such groups initiate lawsuits on behalf of the goals of the movement (Freeman 1975; Pinard 1975).

The black civil rights movement of the 1950s and 1960s benefited from a number of the coalitions. Activists, including members of the Southern Christian Leadership Conference under Martin Luther King, Jr. and followers of the Committee on Racial Equality, acted in cooperation with established interest groups such as the National Association for the Advancement of Colored People (NAACP) in pressing for civil rights goals. The ministers and congregations of many black churches in the South supported the cause of sit–ins, boycotts of segregated public facilities, and other demonstrations, and the black churches served as a communications network that spread the word about the new forms of protest and legitimized them with the black population. The NAACP and later the Leadership Conference on Civil Rights (a Washington, D.C., organization of civil rights lobbyists) lobbied Congress on behalf of the movement activists. Liberal politicians, such as Hubert Humphrey, also advocated the goals of the black protest movement. In other words, existing, established institutions—in this case churches, ethnically oriented associations, and political factions—acted to spread a social movement of sit-in protests, boycotts, marches, demonstrations, etc.

Movement Success In Public Policy

After its ideas become legitimate and widespread, a political movement often achieves a great deal of political success within a short time. At this stage, the movement coalition is able to defeat economic interests and subgovernments which oppose its goals.

Movement Losses In Policy

When the costs of the new public policies instituted by the movement become apparent, the hitherto defeated economic interests, subgovernments, and ideological groups will reassert themselves, gain political strength, and lessen the power of the movement coalition over public policies.

By the time of the Carter and Reagan administrations, the environmentalists, the women's movement, the consumerists, and the government reformers were thrown on the defensive by a newly organized opposition. Perhaps politically the strongest of these movements, environmentalism continued to win substantial victories during the Carter years, such as federal control of strip mining (1977), a continuation of rather strict air pollution controls (1977), and the Alaska Wilderness bill of 1979, which prohibited development of much of that northern state. However, environmentalists were increasingly criticized for contributing to inflation by making economic production more expensive. This criticism provided intellectual justification for a new policy under Reagan and Interior Secretary Watt that gave increased weight to economic considerations in relation to environmental factors in making governmental decisions.

THE CONTINUING TENSION

On balance, theories of the political impact of social movements suggest many limitations to the idea of the American government as a confederation of oligarchies. Yet the idea of oligarchical control remains valid with some considerable qualifications. The pattern of American government may be envisioned as a "checkerboard of oligarchy." There are hundreds of different areas of policy and some of these are controlled by minority factions or iron triangles, which might be represented by the dark squares on the board. Other areas of public policy seem to have broader public participation, and might be represented by lighter shades on the board. Extending the metaphor, one might view various areas of public policy as a growing darker or a growing lighter at a particular time. Public participation in a given area usually varies considerably.

Social movements constitute one type of public participation in politics. They affect decision making by drawing attention to areas of policy that might otherwise attract little interest. Demonstrations, consciousness–raising groups, and various forms of protest may condition public opinion to look favorably upon a movement's goals. Interest groups organize as the movement develops and lobby legislatures for changes in the law or initiate litigation to achieve the same end. Public participation in one or more areas of policy increases and oligarchy or special interest rule decreases. In some cases, skeptics will argue that the new form of policy making is no more democratic than the former practices: Do environmentalists always represent the interests of the majority? Does bargaining with school prayer advocates make school politics more democratic? Nevertheless, social movements involve more people in policy making, and thus have important effects on public policy. While theories of minority faction cannot be discounted, it is likely that the future will bring new social movements to challenge the power of special interests.

Chapter 3

The Role of Religious Organizations in the U.S. Sanctuary Movement

Barbara M. Yarnold

THE ORIGINS OF SOCIAL MOVEMENTS: A PEOPLE'S CHOICE OF NATURAL LAW OVER POSITIVE LAW WHEN THE TWO CONFLICT

Throughout history, there has been a tension between man's adherence to either positive law or natural law. A not uncommon reason for conflict among men and nations has been that one participant in the conflict enacted a written norm or customary practice, or relied upon conventional law in undertaking certain actions, with unjust results. In spite of the argument that the actor's activities conformed with "conventional" or "positive" law, consisting of prevailing laws, norms, or practices, these activities seemed to violate a higher "moral" law, or man's innate "natural law" precepts, which originates either from man's ability to reason or from revelations from God.

Early philosophers were aware of the dichotomy between natural law and positive law. Aristotle, in his *Nichomachean Ethics*, makes a distinction between justice that is natural and justice which is conventional. Conventional justice consists of those written norms which are established by the members of a political society largely due to necessity. Natural justice, on the other hand, consists of those rules which are common among all men according to nature, which are perceived though unwritten, since each man carries within him a conception of justice (Edwards 1981).

Plato served to further articulate the notion of natural law as immutable, and derived from the order of nature. Natural law precepts are aimed at attaining ultimate goodness. Man may find harmony and justice only if he lives in conformity with the truths of nature (Ibid.). In *The Commonwealth*, Cicero, a Roman statesman, followed the lead of the Greek philosophers in postulating the existence of a body of natural law:

There is in fact a true law—namely right reason—which is in accordance with nature, applies to all men, and is unchangeable and eternal. . . . Neither the Senate nor the people can absolve us from our obligation to obey this law, and it requires no Sextus Aelius to expound it and interpret it . . . binding at all times and upon all people; and there will be, as it were, one common master and ruler of men, namely God, who is the author of this law. . . . The man who will not obey it will abandon his better self, and, in denying the true nature of a man, will thereby suffer the severest of penalties, though he has escaped all the other consequences which men call punishment (Ibid.: 29).

There were two distinct schools of thought among early philosophers regarding the origins of natural law. "In the Aristotelian sense, law is the 'right reason' " (Ibid.: 33). It was perceived that through use of his reason, man may become aware of his natural inclinations. Since these natural inclinations are derived from nature, and therefore good, whatever man does in conformity with these natural inclinations is also good. In contrast, anything which hampers a natural inclination is evil.

On the other side of the natural law debate were early Christian philosophers who believed that natural law is only divined by man through his relationship to God. Yet, even when man has an "imperfect" relationship with God, St. Paul recognized that man may still be capable of perceiving some of the dictates of natural law: "For when the Gentiles, which have not the law, do by nature the things contained in the law, these having not the law, are a law unto themselves, which shew the work of laws written in their hearts, their conscience also bearing witness and their thoughts the meanwhile accusing or else excusing one another" (Ibid.: 35).

The contrasting views of natural law as derived from reason or from divine revelation were finally reconciled by St. Thomas Aquinas, who postulated that man's knowledge of natural law is derived from two sources: (1) from nature, in which man is capable of rational discernment of truth, and (2) from supernature, in which man derives truth through divine revelation (Ibid.).

The fact that early Greek, Roman, and Christian philosophers recognized the existence of natural law precepts, which are distinct from conventional or positive law precepts, lends strong support to the argument that an historical tension has existed between man's adherence either to natural or positive law. These writings further suggest that man has a choice between the two, and that it is his responsibility to follow natural law precepts when these conflict with conventional written and unwritten rules, norms, and practices.

To a great extent, social movements which have arisen in the United States may be explained as a collective decision by persons and organizations in the United States to follow natural law over the positive law, when the two conflict.

Social movements have been defined as follows:

. . . a social movement is characterized by activity directed toward changing institutions and behaviors of importance to a society, as opposed to peripheral institutions or routine behaviors. Another defining feature of a social movement is its mode of political expression,

often consisting of unconventional tactics and behavior, such as civil
disobedience, organizing demonstrations, breaking up into small groups
for the purpose of "consciousness raising," and even the threat or actual
use of violence (McFarland 1983: 338).

Hence, social movements call for fundamental change in the
positive law, when the positive law does not coincide with
natural law precepts, and members of social movements are
willing to engage in unconventional tactics to achieve their
goals, even if this means that they must violate positive law.
Andrew McFarland points to a number of social movements
which have existed in the United States during the last three
decades: the civil rights movement, the women's movement,
the governmental reform movement, the consumer protection
movement, the environmental protection movement, the peace
movement, the fundamentalist Christian movement, the tax revolt
movement of 1977–1980, and the "gay rights" movement. Since
McFarland wrote, one new movement may be added to the list,
namely the sanctuary movement. These movements have all
been characterized by a disaffection on the part of movement
participants with the positive law, and a willingness to engage
in nontraditional activity which often contravenes positive law
precepts.

For example, the civil rights movement of the 1950s and early
1960s had a core objective of causing fundamental change in the
positive law of the United States, which allowed for both public
and private discrimination in the United States on the basis of
race (McFarland 1983). Throughout the United States blacks
and whites were segregated; they did not, for example, attend
the same public or private schools, or use the same public or
private accommodations. The law either enforced segregation
of the races (for example, with respect to public schools) or
tacitly failed to interfere with segregation (for example, with
respect to restrictive covenants in leases and other documents).
Various individuals and groups reacted to what appeared to be
an immoral and repugnant positive law, which conflicted with

natural law precepts of justice and equality; their combined actions culminated in what has come to be known as the civil rights movement.

The activities and strategies of participants in the civil rights movement ranged widely, from the legalistic approach of groups like the National Association for the Advancement of Colored People, or NAACP, which fought a laborious battle in state and federal courts to abolish discriminatory laws; to the civil disobedience of followers of the Reverend Martin Luther King, Jr.; to the confrontational, illegal, and often violent strategy employed by groups like the Black Muslims and the Black Panthers (McFarland 1983).

In much the same way, the sanctuary movement which arose in the United States in the early 1980s was a response to what appeared to be an immoral and repugnant positive law which failed to provide refuge to persons from Central American countries. In short, the United States' positive law conflicted with natural law precepts of charity and granting sanctuary to those displaced by natural and man-made disasters. Individuals and organizations responded to this dilemma by making a collective choice in favor of natural law precepts, and in favor of providing these aliens refuge in the United States. Their efforts culminated in the sanctuary movement which is, at its core, an illegal attempt to bypass the legal structures of U.S. immigration laws and procedures. Participants in the sanctuary movement have varied strategies; some participants overtly violate the law, while others offer assistance to more active participants in the movement and the movement's beneficiaries, and remain within the parameters of the positive law.

The impetus to a social movement is collective disaffection with positive law. Hence, the sanctuary movement originated in the frustration of many individuals and organizations in the United States with the failure of U.S. immigration laws to provide refuge to Central Americans fleeing from deteriorating conditions in El Salvador and Guatemala. Both of these countries were torn by civil war, and those who sought shelter in the United States often came with reports of serious human rights abuses, including torture. Refugees from Central America are able, pursuant to U.S. immigration laws, to apply for either political asylum or withholding of deportation on the basis that they have a well-founded fear of persecution or that there is a clear probability that they will be persecuted in their countries of origin. However, many critics note that the immigration bureaucracy favors in refugee and asylum admissions those fleeing from "hostile" countries, defined as countries with communist, socialist or "leftist" forms of government (Preston 1986; Helton 1984; Loescher and Scanlan 1986; Yarnold 1990; Yarnold n.d.). Since both of the Central American countries mentioned—El Salvador and Guatemala—maintain good relations with the United States, aliens from these countries are not likely to be successful applicants for asylum and withholding. Hence, Central American refugees are clearly "refugees without refuge" (Yarnold 1990).

The fact that U.S. immigration law provides no remedy for the vast majority of refugees from Central America has been attested to by many commentators. Among these are individuals within the sanctuary movement, who initially attempted to help Central American refugees through legal immigration channels. These individuals and organizations repeatedly document violations of these aliens' limited due process rights by the immigration bureaucracy in the course of their legal attempts to obtain refuge in the United States. There are also reports that the aliens are often not informed of their right to apply for political asylum and withholding of deportation, or of other statutory and constitutional rights. For example, Susan Gzesch, an immigration attorney who inspected detention camps in Texas, suggests: "The vast majority of Salvadorans are voluntarily returned to their own country by the INS [Immigration and Naturalization Service] without ever having had the opportunity to apply for political asylum. Many of them return never knowing such an opportunity exists, or if they did know, they were discouraged from applying by INS authorities, who see their primary work as returning undocumented entrants quickly" (Golden and McConnell 1986: 41).

Renny Golden and Michael McConnell claim that lawyers working through immigration channels on behalf of Central American refugees had "documented violations of due process so consistent as to constitute a policy" (Ibid.).

Of course, due process and other violations on the part of the immigration bureaucracy with respect to asylum and withholding applicants from El Salvador and Guatemala would not be as significant if these aliens were obtaining substantive relief. This is not, however, the case. Most aliens from these countries who apply for either type of relief are unsuccessful. Golden and McConnell comment: "Even if allowed to apply for political asylum, however, Central Americans rarely are granted asylum. More statistics show that nationwide over twenty-two thousand applied during 1982; only seventy-four were granted asylum. For the year 1984, out of thirteen thousand Salvadoran asylum requests, only 325 were granted" (Ibid.: 42).

These commentators also suggest that a lack of publicly available information about background conditions in these countries—El Salvador and Guatemala—keeps most people in the United States uninformed about the conditions in which Central American refugees, deported to their countries of origin, are forced to live. Hence, public opinion in the United States has not yet risen to the level of opposing current practices of the immigration bureaucracy with respect to its treatment of these refugees, and public pressure is not likely to force policy changes in this area. Further, both private citizens and policymakers in the United States are, according to these authors, intentionally misinformed about conditions in El Salvador, Gautemala, and Honduras, since most government reports indicate that human rights abuses in these countries are diminishing and that these countries are even engaging in democratization when many suggest conditions have either remained the same or have deteriorated.

In response to an inability to obtain natural law goals through the mechanism of the positive law, persons and organizations in the United States who became involved in the sanctuary movement increasingly abandoned resort to the positive law. Some went beyond this, however, and actively violated the law in order to provide refuge to Central American refugees. One such individual, who can safely be referred to as one of the founders of the United States sanctuary movement, is Jim Corbett who, according to most accounts, was the first in the United States to bring a Central American refugee across the border to safety. This took place in the spring of 1981, when Corbett transported a Salvadoran from the Mexican border to John Fife's Presbyterian church in Tucson, Arizona. John Fife explains how he came to resort to the illegal harboring of aliens in his church:

Initially we were involved with undocumented people, raising bond money, and getting lawyers to assist people who had already been arrested by the INS. We had been doing this for six months or so. Well, I am not mentally retarded and after that much involvement with legal defense efforts, I realized that they were neither effective nor moral. After a while it became apparent that this was an exercise in futility. You recognize very quickly that nobody is going to get asylum except a tiny minority (*Catholic Agitator* 1984).

Jim Corbett was one of the first in the sanctuary movement to encourage others to abandon reliance on the positive law in this area in exchange for adherence only to moral precepts, or natural law. For example, in an article submitted to the National Lawyers Guild's Central American Refugee Defense Fund Newsletter, dated June 6, 1986, Corbett wrote:

The defense of human rights by the church is faith-based and worship initiated, but we need look neither to heaven, nor to the Bible nor to corporate conscience for the higher law that overrules unjust laws. The community that dedicates itself to doing justice exposes and challenges an outlaw administration in ways that simple resistance to injustice does not, because compliance with human rights law that is being violated by the state requires that a community assume on-going administrative functions that breach the regulatory "territory" assigned to government officials . . . concerning the screening, placement, and protection of Central American refugees, for example, the sanctuary network is an emergency alternative to the INS (1986: 3).

At another time, Corbett explained resort to illegality as follows: "When the government itself sponsors the torture of entire peoples and then makes it a felony to shelter those seeking refuge, law-abiding protest merely trains us to live with atrocity. The presence of undocumented refugees here among us makes the definitive nature of our choice particularly clear and concrete. Where oppression rules, the way of peace is necessarily insurgent" (Golden and McConnell 1986: 37).

In fact, the route chosen by Corbett seemed to be more effective than a purely legal one. By 1984, Corbett had brought 700 Central American refugees into the United States. At the same time, few Central American refugees who pursued legal channels obtained asylum or withholding.

Ted Loder, Senior Minister of the First United Methodist Church of Germantown, a church in Philadelphia which provided sanctuary for a Guatemalan refugee family, also writes of the choice he faced when confronted with an immoral positive law: "Still, to be human at all, you—I—have to make moral choices and take moral actions. The evidence, incomplete as it may be, is persuasive that some things are simply wrong. Injustice, exploitation, oppression, tyranny are arguably real in our common life, even if the solutions are arguable. The whisper—or scream— of conscience can be ignored only at peril to one's humanity" (Loder 1986: 38–39).

The comments of those involved in the sanctuary movement in the United States suggest that their choice to resort to illegal acts, acts which contravene the positive law, was compelled by their greater loyalty to moral or natural law precepts. As suggested earlier, social movements generally originate from conflict between principles of positive and natural law.

COMMUNICATION OF IDEAS OF A SOCIAL MOVEMENT BY INTEREST GROUPS— EXAMINATION IN THE CONTEXT OF THE U.S. SANCTUARY MOVEMENT

One of the most significant "links" between social movements and organized interest groups is that organized interests may act as a "communications network" for social movements, facilitating the communication of major ideas of social movements in a way that may legitimize movements, bring public pressure for policy change to the fore, attract entrepreneurial politicians who adopt all or part of a social movement's platform, and effect policy change (McFarland 1983; Freeman 1975). Thus, social movements are dependent upon organized interests; the failure of organized interests to communicate any of the ideas of a social movement may result in the failure of the social movement to cause any significant policy change.

One question which arises relates to which interest groups are likely to act as the essential "link" between the ideas of a social movement and a political system. It is suggested that there are various types of interest groups which, it can be imagined, form and maintain concentric circles around a political system. Those interest groups which are the most dependent upon the political system and whose structure and activities are largely shaped by the political system are not likely to be the first to embrace the ideas of a social movement, particularly when the participants in a social movement resort to illegal modes of conduct. This first layer of organizations will be referred to as "entrenched organizations." By use of this term, it is stressed that these organizations have become, in a significant way, a part of the political system. Entrenched organizations adhere primarily to positive law precepts, even when these conflict with moral or natural law precepts. Like government agencies, the main objective of these organizations has become, in spite of previous orientations, organizational maintenance. To the extent that identification with the non-mainstream policies of a social movement and with the illegal activities of participants in a social movement may jeopardize the reputation and financial resources available to entrenched organizations, they are not likely to be the first to adopt the ideas of a social movement. Such organizations may only become involved in promoting the ideas of a social movement after these ideas have been legitimized and publicized by other interest groups and politicians.

Entrenched organizations are of two types: (1) social welfare organizations, and (2) legal organizations. For reasons that will be discussed at a later point, legal interest groups may be far less amenable to the ideas of a social movement than social welfare interest groups.

Although there are obviously groups which fall between the layers, for the sake of simplicity, the second layer of interest groups which are identified will be referred to as "fringe organizations." It is expected that fringe organizations provide the important communication system for the ideas of a social movement. Fringe organizations tend to be less dependent on the political system for support, structure, and shaping of the strategies employed by the organizations. Unlike entrenched organizations, which are primarily oriented toward organizational maintenance, fringe organizations are primarily policy oriented, pursuing policy goals even when this interferes with organizational maintenance. Fringe organizations tend to follow moral or natural law precepts when these conflict with positive law precepts. Fringe organizations do not have the same "stake" in the political system as entrenched organizations. Hence, for example, fringe organizations may adopt the ideas of a social movement more readily than entrenched organizations, even when a social movement's ideas and conduct are unconventional, since fringe organizations do not have to protect established reputations for the sake of maintaining financial support.

Fringe Organizations

Fringe organizations are motivated by natural law concepts, and often promote these concepts in a manner that not only conflicts with the positive law but, also, directly violates it. Fringe organizations are more responsive to the natural law precepts advanced by a social movement than are entrenched organizations, which are based in positive law. Fringe organizations do not strive for organizational maintenance to the same extent as entrenched organizations, and for this reason, their continued existence tends to be constantly in question. Due to their adoption of unpopular policy positions and, often, modes of conduct, these organizations may have difficulty attracting and maintaining financial support from government, business, private foundations, other organizations, and other sources which are established and have a stake in the larger political system. Hence, fringe organizations may be of limited duration, and may encounter official and unofficial resistance which limits their ability to pursue their policy goals.

The most significant point to note with respect to fringe organizations is that these organizations are often the first or only "voice" of a social movement. Hence, these organizations provide social movements with a communications system that alerts other organizations, policymakers, and the general public to the core ideas of the social movement (Freeman 1975). The following discussion examines fringe organizations, both religious and secular.

Religious "Fringe" Organizations

History is replete with examples of religious organizations which have come into conflict with positive law due to their adherence to their perception of a higher, moral law. In the United States, various religious organizations actively engage in efforts to either change the existing positive law or interfere with its administration. For example, particularly in the late 1980s and early 1990s, anti-abortion church groups have engaged in systematic lobbying efforts designed to replace laws which allowed women to obtain abortions with laws that prohibit abortions. Some of these religious organizations, however, went beyond legal mechanisms when legal methods failed. Hence, for example, members of religious organizations engaged in sit-ins at abortion clinics, obstructive picketing, and even bombing of clinics. Their justification for these "extralegal" and "nonlegal" methods was that they were seeking to promote a natural law precept—protection of the unborn—which takes precedence over conflicting positive law precepts.

To the extent that religious organizations adhere to natural law precepts over the positive law, they share much in common with participants in social movements. Religious organizations have been rather hospitable to social movements, adopting the major policy positions of movements and serving to communicate these ideas to the general public, other organizations, and policymakers. Since the 1950s, for example, religious organizations have acted as communications systems for the civil rights movement, the peace movement, and the fundamentalist Christian movement, among others (McFarland 1983). Due to their historic commitment to natural law, religious organizations generally play an important role in social movements, unless the core ideas of social movements conflict with the religious dogma of these organizations. The identification of religious organizations with the ideas of a social movement gives to these ideas a measure of legitimacy.

Religious organizations which have become involved in social movements are properly classified as "fringe" organizations. Crucial to their independence from political systems is that they rarely rely, to a great extent, on government subsidies for support, or upon private foundations, wealthy individuals, business and professional organizations, and other interests which are "entrenched"—that is, have a great stake in the existing political and economic systems. Instead, religious organizations are supported primarily by their congregations. Hence, these organizations are not concerned with maintaining a reputation for seeking conventional policy goals and engaging in conventional political activity in order to ensure their continued financial support by government or persons and organizations entrenched in the existing political and economic system. Of course, this is not to suggest that these religious organizations are impervious to the political system. In the United States, for example, church organizations active in the sanctuary movement feared loss of tax-exempt status, and criminal indictments against members of the organizations who were active in the sanctuary movement. In spite of these penalties, religious organizations continue to advance natural law precepts.

A prime example of the communication link between fringe religious organizations and social movements arises in the context of the civil rights movement. During the early 1950s, black Protestant churches were used to communicate the ideas of the civil rights movement. The acknowledged leader of the civil rights movement, Dr. Martin Luther King, Jr., was a Baptist minister. In these religious organizations, ministers appealed to a higher, moral law which contrasted sharply with a positive law which allowed for both *de facto* and *de jure* discrimination against blacks. The civil rights movement was communicated through the churches to blacks, who then engaged in protests, civil disobedience, and in some instances, violent activity. Through these acts, the larger white population became informed of the major ideas of the civil rights movement. Policy changes were to occur after the adoption of some of the major precepts of the social movement by both "entrenched" persons and organizations (such as the American Civil Liberties Union) and political entrepreneurs, such as President Lyndon B. Johnson (McFarland 1983).

The independence of black churches which acted as spokesmen for the central ideas of the civil rights movement was attributable to the fact that they were not dependent on any governmental unit for financial support, nor upon established interests, such as other organizations, wealthy contributors, private foundations, and business organizations. Their activity was subsidized by contributions from church members.

The sanctuary movement which arose in the United States in the early 1980s provides an even better example of the communication "link" between fringe religious organizations and the ideas of a social movement than does the civil rights movement of the 1950s since the sanctuary movement is a church-initiated movement, which attracted little support from non-religious organizations. The religious base of the sanctuary movement is best illustrated by the following statement, contained in an informational pamphlet distributed by the Chicago Religious Task Force on Central America (CRTFCA), in February 1988 (CRTFCA is the national coordinating body for the sanctuary movement):

We believe that God's revelation is principally discovered among the world's oppressed and most vulnerable. Both the Torah and the Gospel compel us to choose sides with the poor, creating a covenant of solidarity with those struggling for life and justice. God chose to act decisively for the liberation of the Hebrews from bondage in Egypt. The prophets continually advocated for the rights of the poor, sojourners, widows, and orphans. The ministry of Jesus began with the proclamation to "set free those who are oppressed."

In a June 1987 edition of *Basta*, a journal produced by CRTFCA, Jon Sobrino (1987) discusses the theological justification for the sanctuary movement:

The sanctuary movement is theologically justified because it is a way of defending the lives of the poor and thus of believing in and responding to the God of Christian biblical faith. The central theological thesis is the following: God is the defender of the lives of the poor and makes that defense something ultimate, unconditional and higher than everything else; every human being and, therefore, all believers especially have the right and the obligation to defend the lives of the poor (19–20).

By December 1987, *Basta* reported that there were 448 sanctuary locations in the United States. Of these, 405, or slightly over 90 percent, were organized either by religious congregations (404) or by seminaries (1). Only 43, or 10 percent, were organized by non-religious entities, including cities (27) and universities (16) (*Basta* 12/87: 2).

Sanctuary has a long historical tradition in both Christian and Jewish history. During World War II Protestant and Catholic churches throughout the world gave refuge to Jews persecuted by Germans. These historical precedents gave the sanctuary movement carried on by religious organizations additional legitimacy and urgency. Participants in the sanctuary movement chose natural law precepts over positive law precepts, and chose to violate the positive law when this appeared necessary.

For some time after the sanctuary movement was launched by Jim Corbett in 1981, it remained a local phenomenon, based out of John Fife's church in Tucson, and supported by the Tucson Ecumenical Council, a coalition of sixty Tucson churches. Before adopting illegal strategies, Corbett and the Tucson Ecumenical Council attempted legal strategies for helping aliens from Guatemala, Honduras, and El Salvador. At one point, their joint efforts raised $100,000 for a bailout of Central American refugees kept in a regional detention center. Ultimately, their efforts to help these aliens through legal channels failed. Of the one hundred refugees they had "bonded out," only 5 percent were able to obtain political asylum. In order to raise the sum of $100,000, ministers and members of congregations mortgaged their homes. The Tucson group came to agree:

There is no justice for Central American refugees under present INS policy and with present State Department and INS personnel. The system and the foreign policy that controls it are misconceived. For any church or agency to encourage refugees to voluntarily enter this system, other than as a last resort, would be at best a mistake, and at worst, complicity in the violation of human rights. Evasion services, sanctuary, and an extensive underground railroad were the answer (Golden and McConnell 1986: 46).

Michael McConnell (1986: 9) comments in a June 1986 edition of *Basta*: "the Sanctuary Movement began in 1982 in direct response to the refugees fleeing the violence and death squad killings in El Salvador and Guatemala." The first pastor in the United States to publicly declare that his church was a sanctuary was Reverend John Fife in March 1982. Shortly after, five East Bay churches in California were also declared places of sanctuary.

Soon after these proclamations, however, the resources of the early sanctuary churches were severely tapped. Leaders of the sanctuary movement increasingly sought to make the movement national in scope. In August 1982, CRTFCA, then a coalition of local religious groups, accepted its first Central American refugees. Corbett approached the organization and requested that it become the national coordinator of the underground railroad. CRTFCA accepted his offer, and is currently occupying this leadership position in the sanctuary movement (Golden and McConnell 1986).

After this point, according to Golden and McConnell: "from coast to coast a railroad would extend as far north as Canada and as far east as Boston" (Ibid.: 52). The number of religious organizations which offered sanctuary to Central American refugees, according to one account, numbered only 30 in 1982 (Golden and McConnell 1986: 53). By December 1987, *Basta* reported a total of 448 sanctuary locations nationwide; over 90 percent of these are affiliated with religious organizations (*Basta* 12/87: 2). The increase in sanctuary sites demonstrates that the sanctuary movement has grown from a local phenomenon to a social movement that is national in scope. In fact, the sanctuary movement even transcends national boundaries. Through links with sanctuary providers in Central America and Canada, which also tend to be religious organizations, the sanctuary movement has become international in scope (*Basta* 9/86: 3–4).

Basta lists the following as the goals of the sanctuary movement: "To protect as many as possible of the refugees whom conscience demands we not allow our government to deport; to let our witness function as pressure against inhumane policies which both create refugees and then deny them haven" (9/86: 14).

By September 1986, *Basta* was reporting that the second goal, that of publicizing the plight of refugees and changing public policy in the United States, had failed: "after four years, Sanctuary and the U.S. undeclared war in Central America is not a national issue. Information and debate on Central America has not reached a mass level" (9/86: 13).

Robin Semer, a staff member of CRTFCA, in a March 3, 1988 interview, indicated that the sanctuary movement had helped thousands of Central American refugees. She conceded that this was a minute fraction of Central American refugees in need of assistance, but suggested that Central American refugees who came to the United States and found sanctuary alerted United States religious congregations and the public to the intolerable conditions in Central American countries.

Nevertheless, a contributor to *Basta*, Archbishop Rivera y Damas, reaffirmed commitment to the sanctuary movement in December 1986, in spite of its partial failure: "Sanctuary will continue as long as the war in Central America continues to bomb civilians, abuse the rights of citizens and create refugees and displaced persons. Only when the war ends and El Salvador and Guatemala are sanctuaries for their people will the Sanctuary Movement stop" (12/86: 25).

Individuals and religious organizations who were engaged in smuggling aliens from Central America into the United States, transporting them, and harboring them were violating federal statutes which prohibit these actions. In February 1984, the first arrests of members of the sanctuary movement were made, of Stacey Merkdt and Dianne Muhlenkamp. In April 1984, Jack Elder was also arrested; all three were affiliated with Casa Romero, a Central American refugee assistance center sponsored by the Catholic Church, located near the Rio Grande. After her arrest, Stacey Merkdt wrote: "How long can we close our eyes to the 'disappeareds,' to the continued increase in killing, to the torture and to the Salvadoran government's participation in this? Who is the criminal? Who will allow it to continue?" (Golden and McConnell 1986: 68).

A contributor to *Basta* made the following summary of the so-called "Tucson trial":

The government's short-term tactic, criminal conviction, was temporarily successful in pure result-oriented terms. Eight of eleven people were convicted on 18 of 71 original charges. . . . However, the convictions were extracted at great cost. Sanctuary supporters, along with most defendants, experienced their first taste of the U.S. justice system: its operation was not fair (9/86: 23).

The conclusion of this contributor to *Basta* is as follows: "The fundamental lesson, as always, is that only organized movements cause change. The legal system is another branch of the political system that we must use toward the end of justice at every turn. But as our history teaches us, the legal system often lags behind morality and justice" (Ibid.: 25).

These statements are typical of those produced by individuals and religious organizations who participate in the sanctuary movement. There is a willingness to violate the positive law when this is necessary to meet the demands of natural law. The religious organizations which became involved in the sanctuary movement are properly described as "fringe" organizations since they were loyal to natural law precepts, not positive law precepts, and they did not have a reputation to uphold for the purpose of securing contributions from the government or other "entrenched" interests which had flourished in the existing political and economic system and thus had a stake in the maintenance of the status quo. The independence of religious organizations may be attributed to the fact that they received most of their support from their congregations. The independence of fringe religious organizations, however, is not without cost. They have often met with official and unofficial repression. Supporters of sanctuary claim that sanctuary workers have had to contend with criminal indictments, break-ins at churches, suspected telephone taps, and arrests of refugees (Ibid.: 23).

Religious organizations involved in the sanctuary movement are policy-oriented, and unlike entrenched organizations, have not directed much attention to organizational maintenance. Since these religious organizations initiated, and attempt to carry out, the agenda of the sanctuary movement, they have served as an important communications system, communicating the core ideas of the movement to other organizations, to the general public, and to public policymakers.

One of the most important mechanisms through which the ideas of any social movement, including the sanctuary movement, are communicated to other sectors of society is the media.

Members of religious fringe organizations which support the sanctuary movement and are active participants in it have made use of the media as a communications tool, through contacting members of the press whenever an affiliate organization offered sanctuary to refugees from Central America, and through inviting press coverage of the trials of participants in the sanctuary movement.

Although these efforts have not yet had a significant impact upon U.S. policy with respect to the governments of El Salvador and Guatemala, or upon U.S. policy with respect to refugees from these countries, the fact that the number of religious and secular organizations which provide sanctuary to Central American refugees, an illegal act, has increased from 30 in 1982 to 448 in December 1987 indicates that the core ideas of the sanctuary movement have been adopted by some segments of American society. Most important is the fact that the concept of sanctuary has gained the support of religious leaders from the largest religious organizations in the United States (including Baptist, Brethren, Disciples of Christ, Episcopalian, Jewish, New Jewish Agenda, Lutheran, Mennonite, Methodist, Presbyterian, Quaker, Roman Catholic, United Church of Christ, Unitarian Universalist, other Protestant, and Ecumenical), since these religious leaders have an existing communications system through which they may spread the ideas of the sanctuary movement to their congregations and, hence, the general public (McFarland 1983). If the public comes to support a more even-handed application of the laws relating to refugees and asylees from these countries, "political entrepreneurs" may attempt to garner electoral support by adopting the policy platform of the sanctuary movement.

By March 1988, CRTFCA staffer Semer suggested that media attention to the sanctuary movement had diminished. She predicted that the sanctuary movement will "exist but not flourish." When most social movements fade from public consciousness, donations to movement organizations decrease and, as a result, the social movement wanes (McFarland 1983).

One feature of the sanctuary movement, however, which distinguishes it from other social movements and gives it an additional measure of "survivability" is that it is, for the most part, church-based, and thus has a constant source of organizational support. Other social movements, such as the consumer protection movement, tended to wane as public attention came to focus upon other policy issues and movement organizations began to see their supply of funds diminish. In contrast, religious organizations that support the sanctuary movement have a constant source of support from members of their congregations who contribute to the support of the religious organizations, and not specifically to support sanctuary movement goals. Leaders of these religious organizations may continue to press for the goals of the sanctuary movement even after public support for the movement dissipates. Hence, the sanctuary movement is likely to have a semi-perpetual existence, losing impetus not due to a lack of financial and organizational support, but due to a loss of interest on the part of religious leaders.

Secular "Fringe" Organizations

Secular "fringe" organizations share in common with religious "fringe" organizations a number of characteristics. First is their adherence to natural law, or moral concepts, over positive law. Second is their willingness to engage in acts ranging from legal conduct to civil disobedience to violent activity which contravenes the positive law, in order to advance natural law objectives. These organizations, like their religious counterparts, do not depend heavily on government for financial support. Nor do they depend heavily on contributions from persons and organizations which have benefitted from the political and economic system operating within the United States, such as private foundations, private corporations, business and professional organizations, and wealthy individuals. Instead, secular fringe organizations tend to rely on small budgets; their funds may be donated by individuals who are supportive of their objectives. Like religious fringe organizations, their primary objective is to

promote policy goals, and not to ensure organizational maintenance. These organizations also play an important role in communicating the ideas of a social movement, though perhaps in a
more sporadic fashion than fringe religious organizations. They
tend to be disadvantaged relative to their religious counterparts,
which have a measure of legitimacy in the United States simply
due to their status as religious organizations.

Hence, for example, the objectives of the civil rights movement
were also advanced by such groups as the Black Panther and Black
Muslim organizations, and members of these organizations were
informed by their leadership of the main goals of the civil rights
movement. However, when these organizations resorted to illegal
activity, the response was swift and severe. Within a short time
after its formation, for example, the Black Panther group was
deprived, due to criminal convictions and official surveillance,
of effective leadership. After some time, the Black Panther
organization abandoned most of its far-reaching goals and came to
act much like a social welfare agency. Although its independence
from the government and entrenched interests provided the Black
Panthers with the ability to engage in unconventional conduct and
support unpopular policy positions, this independence was also,
in part, responsible for its demise.

The sanctuary movement has also been supported by a number
of secular "fringe organizations," which serve to communicate the
major ideas of the movement. These secular fringe organizations,
like religious fringe organizations, have a natural law orientation
and pursue natural law objectives even when this means that
participants violate the positive law.

One such "fringe" secular group is the Pledge of Resistance
(POR), which was organized nationwide in 1984 " . . . in response to the escalation of U.S. intervention in the war in Central
America" (CRTFCA 1988). The Pledge of Resistance was formed
for the purpose of carrying out acts of civil disobedience, aimed
at gaining media attention and public support for the goals of
the sanctuary movement. Although the POR is independent
from CRTFCA, CRTFCA coordinates the POR in Chicago.

An information pamphlet distributed by CRTFCA in February 1988 discusses the activities of the POR in Chicago:

The Chicago Pledge of Resistance has done numerous creative actions. It has organized against the passage of contra aid, the bombings in El Salvador and U.S. government and press disinformation on Central America; presently, it is organizing around stopping the deployment of the Illinois National Guard to Central America. At the same time, the Pledge responds to emergencies as they occur.

Some of the "creative actions" engaged in by the Chicago POR include a March 1985 sit-in at Senator Alan Dixon's office after he voted in favor of contra aid; nine members of the POR were arrested. That month the Chicago POR conducted a month-long vigil in the Federal Plaza, with flowerpots dedicated to persons "martyred" in Central America. In September 1985, members of the Chicago POR demonstrated against U.S. involvement in El Salvador by appearing inside a United States Air Force recruiting station in Chicago; five persons were arrested. In November 1985, members of the Chicago POR staged a mock trial and a prayer service in support of eleven sanctuary workers involved in the "Tucson trial"; 200 persons entered a federal building in Chicago and 40 remained, risking arrest (*Basta* 12/85: 3–5).

The Pledge of Resistance is committed to civil disobedience due to its concern for natural law principles, namely to "halt the death and destruction which U.S. military action cause the people of Central America" (CRTFCA 1988). The Pledge of Resistance has opened offices throughout the United States. The POR's acts of civil disobedience have met with official reaction in the form of arrests, indictments, and criminal convictions. It is too early to say whether the POR will have a significant impact upon the opinion of the U.S. public relating to U.S. policy toward El Salvador and Guatemala, and refugees from these countries. However, the POR, as a secular "fringe" organization, is likely to have less impact upon public perceptions and policy than religious

"fringe" organizations active in the sanctuary movement, due
to the fact that the POR lacks an established communications
system that religious organizations typically have, as well as the
organizational and financial resources and inherent legitimacy of
religious "fringe" organizations. The POR will probably have a
shorter life span than religious "fringe" organizations active in
the sanctuary movement.

Entrenched Organizations

At an earlier point in the discussion, "entrenched" organizations were distinguished from "fringe" organizations on the
basis of the adherence of entrenched organizations to positive
law precepts, as opposed to natural law precepts, which are
the domain of fringe organizations. Entrenched organizations
are, in a very meaningful way, a part of the political system
in which they operate, and dependent upon the status quo.
Their financial support is garnered from government and private
corporations, business and professional organizations, private
foundations, wealthy contributors: individuals and groups which
have an interest in maintaining the current political and economic
environment.

As a result, entrenched organizations are quite conscious of
their reputations, and avoid taking unpopular policy positions
or engaging in conduct that contravenes the positive law. Their
link to the political system defines the strategies and actions
these organizations pursue, which are, for the most part, set by
political and economic structures. Hence, for example, entrenched
organizations engage in providing social and legal services, and
utilize conventional modes of altering public policy. Entrenched
organizations, unlike fringe organizations, are primarily committed to organizational maintenance. Typically, entrenched organizations are not the first groups to communicate the ideas of a
social movement. This task is left, instead, to fringe organizations.
Entrenched organizations only come to support the major ideas of
a social movement after those ideas have gained popular attention

and perhaps, support from the public or political entrepreneurs.

There are two major types of "entrenched" organizations: those which provide social services and those which provide legal services.

Entrenched Organizations Which Provide Social Services

This category of entrenched organizations which provide social services includes organizations such as the United Way and the United States Catholic Conference. They are "entrenched" due to their dependence upon grants from federal, state, and local governments and due to the generally cooperative arrangements they have entered into with government. This category of social services providers includes both secular and religious organizations, but they share in common a commitment to adhering to the positive law; to acting in a legal and, for the most part, uncontroversial manner.

Organizations such as these have not become meaningfully involved in the sanctuary movement, except indirectly. They may supply social services to refugees from Central America who have found refuge in a sanctuary in the United States, but this is not an organizational objective. These organizations do not actively engage in communicating the ideas of the sanctuary movement nor do they act as advocates of those Central American refugees they serve.

Entrenched Organizations Which Provide Legal Services

Entrenched organizations which provide legal services share most of the characteristics of entrenched organizations which provide social services. They are dependent upon maintenance of the status quo since they obtain their financial resources to a great extent from entrenched interests, including: federal, state, and local government; bar associations; business organizations; private foundations; law schools; and wealthy individuals. Their main loyalty is to the positive law, even when it conflicts with natural law precepts. Hence, action pursued by these organizations tends to be uniformly legal. The tendency toward legality is even more pronounced in entrenched organizations that offer legal services. Their main activity—litigation—negates the possibility of nonlegal conduct. Social movements, such as the sanctuary movement, which rely to a great extent on nonlegal conduct and whose adherents claim that the legal system does not provide relief, threaten the existence of legal organizations. In fact, social movements, including the sanctuary movement, are often justified on the basis that the legal system is largely unresponsive to the ideas of the social movement or the individuals represented by the social movement. An obvious implication is that legal interest groups thus serve no legitimate function, aside from preserving the status quo.

Since entrenched legal interest groups are primarily interested in organizational maintenance and not in effecting major changes in public policy, it is not surprising that a natural antipathy often arises between entrenched legal interest groups and participants in social movements. For example, most (37, or 64 percent) of the legal interest groups interviewed in 1988—59 total sample organizations— (Yarnold 1990) which provide services to aliens who seek political asylum or withholding of deportation on the basis that they are "refugees," indicated that they had no interaction whatsoever with persons in the sanctuary movement in spite of the fact that they regularly represent Central Americans who seek asylum and withholding. Some of the organizational representatives even expressed outright hostility toward the sanctuary movement, indicating that they encourage refugees from Central America to attempt to obtain relief through the legal system, rather than through the illegal mechanism of sanctuary. This is surprising, given the fact that few, if any of these organizations indicated that they have significant success in representing Central American refugees before the immigration bureaucracy. There was, however, a group of entrenched legal services interest groups (21, or 36 percent of the sample) which is less "entrenched" or established than others and indicated that they cooperate to some extent with members of the sanctuary movement through, for example, providing legal representation to Central American refugees referred by sanctuary churches or by helping sanctuary churches obtain the release of Central American refugees held in detention facilities. One such organization was Proyecto Libertad, located in Harlingen, Texas. It is interesting to note that entrenched legal organizations which did have contact with the sanctuary movement tended to be younger, less estabblished, and less well-known than legal services organizations which never had contact with the sanctuary movement. In addition, legal services organizations that had contact with the sanctuary movement tended to be less stable financially than those with no such contact, depending to a greater extent on donations from churches, and uncertain about the source and existence of future funding (Yarnold 1990).

It should be noted, however, that even those entrenched legal organizations which had contact with the sanctuary movement did not abandon their commitment to seeking only legal channels of relief for Central American refugees. This is not to say, of course, that entrenched organizations never promote movement goals and communicate these goals. Freeman (1975) shows that though groups within the women's liberation movement were often divided, radical feminist groups and more conservative groups such as Women's Equity Action League (WEAL) worked together toward a movement goal of promoting women's equality and also served to communicate the ideas of the movement.

The relationship between entrenched legal interest groups and fringe sanctuary organizations in the refugee/asylum policy area is somewhat exceptional. Fringe organizations within the sanctuary movement, by placing primary emphasis on illegal means of assisting refugees and asylees, directly challenge the legitimacy of entrenched legal interest groups.

Nevertheless, even in the ordinary case, entrenched groups are limited in their advocacy of policy goals by the fact that they are dependent upon other entrenched interests and perhaps government for their support. If they take a policy position which is too diverse from that taken by organizations which support them, these entrenched organizations will likely lose their support. Hence, in deciding between taking an unpopular policy position and ensuring organizational maintenance, entrenched organizations which continue to exist have likely favored organizational maintenance. Not surprisingly, entrenched legal organizations do not serve as effective communicators of the major ideas of the sanctuary movement.

PROLIFERATION OF INTEREST GROUPS— EXAMINATION IN THE CONTEXT OF THE U.S. SANCTUARY MOVEMENT

Another important aspect of social movements relates to a social movement's ability to increase countervailing power through the proliferation of interest groups in the course of a movement (McFarland 1987; Freeman 1975).

The sanctuary movement, for example, has coincided with an increase in interest groups which assist refugees from Central America. The Central America Resource Center in Austin, Texas, has published, since 1984, a *Directory of Central America Organizations*, consisting of a list of organizations which offer assistance to Central American refugees nationwide.

The 1984 edition of the Directory lists 400 to 425 "Central America" organizations; the 1985 Directory lists 850 organizations; by 1987 (Third Edition) 1,070 "Central America" organizations were included in the Directory (Central America Resource Center 1984, 1985, 1987). The Central America organizations are grouped into the following categories: refugee legal assistance, refugee sanctuary, research, solidarity, speakers, and travel. In each year since the Directory was issued, the number of organizations in each category has increased. This provides indirect support for the hypothesis that the sanctuary movement has led to the formation of new interest groups, which provide legal services, social services, advocacy, and sanctuary to Central American refugees.

Earlier in this analysis, the increase in the number of sanctuary locations for refugees from Central America was also noted; from 30 in 1982 to 448 in December 1987 (most of which are made available by religious organizations), and the simultaneous mobilization of secular "fringe" organizations including, for example, the Pledge of Resistance.

The 59 entrenched legal services organizations mentioned earlier are also instructive; most of the organizations which assisted aliens in asylum-related appeals to the Board of Immigration Appeals (BIA) and the federal courts are relatively "new" organizations, formed in or after 1980 (Yarnold 1990).

The theoretical importance of the fact that the sanctuary movement spawned the growth of new interest groups is that, in doing so, it also served to increase countervailing power against the U.S. policy of barring the entry of Salvadoran and Guatemalan refugees, and in denying that these aliens are political, and not economic, refugees.

Countervailing power produced by social movements tends to decrease when social movements wane, and public support for the movement and movement organizations diminishes. However, the sanctuary movement is unusual in that countervailing power may not wane even if public support for sanctuary diminishes. This is due to the fact that the sanctuary movement is largely the product of religious groups which have independent financial and organizational resources necessary to sustain the movement even in the absence of popular support.

CONCLUSION

The sanctuary movement, like social movements generally, was the product of a collective decision on the part of (primarily religious) individuals and groups in favor of natural law precepts over the positive law when the two were in conflict. U.S. refugee and asylum policy, or the positive law, serves both to limit immigration flows and to favor in refugee admissions aliens from hostile countries of origin. Individuals and "fringe" organizations in the United States chose to follow natural law precepts and violate the positive law by sheltering Central American refugees in the United States in violation of the law. "Fringe" religious and secular organizations carried the sanctuary movement forward with little direct assistance from "entrenched" organizations, which rely for their support on other "entrenched" interests and government. "Fringe" sanctuary organizations, which based their resort to illegal channels on the illegitimacy of political and legal structures in the United States, directly challenge the existence of "entrenched" legal interest groups. "Entrenched" organizations were not particularly effective in communicating the ideas of the sanctuary movement.

The sanctuary movement also seemed to spawn new interest groups, dedicated to assisting refugees and asylees. The U.S. policy of limiting immigration flows and favoring hostile state aliens thus led to a countermobilization of public interest groups oriented toward helping refugees and asylees. These groups operate both within and outside the parameters of the legal system.

Chapter 4

The Role of Religious Organizations in the Peace Movement Between the Wars

William R. Marty

Christians, in their actions in the world, are like others. Sometimes their actions are wise and morally appropriate, sometimes not. Christians, for example, were enormously important in the abolition movement in this nation, and in the attempt in Britain to end the international slave trade. Christians were important, too, in the civil rights movement in this nation in the critical decades—in leadership positions, in the formation of important organizations, and in providing support. But not all Christian initiatives have been as successful and appropriate. One that was not was the development, between the world wars, of a new kind of pacifism. It is a tale worth telling, because this is a path we may be tempted to tread again.

THREE TRADITIONS ON WAR AND PEACE

Religious organizations within the Christian tradition have operated within three broad traditions on the questions of war and peace: pacifism, just war theory, and the crusade. Pacifism is the earliest of these traditions. For almost two centuries, Christians everywhere were pacifists (Ramsey 1961: xv).[1] The reasons for this were many; Paul Ramsey provided a list. It included the exemption of all Jews (including the Christian sect who would not fight on the Sabbath) from Roman military service; the avoidance of military service to avoid idolatrous emperor-worship (cf. Nuttall 1958); anti-imperialism; the association of military service with devotion to the things of this world; the separation of early Christians in a large empire from positions of political power and responsibility; and the expectation of the imminent return of Christ (Ramsey 1961: xvff; Bainton 1960). It included, as well, an attempt to act in accordance with what were understood to be the implications of Christian love (Ramsey 1961: xvi). But those implications, of necessity, had to be a matter of interpretation, for the Gospels did not provide a set of legalistic commands on the subject. Thus Roland Bainton, who was sympathetic to pacifism, agreed with Paul Ramsey, who was sympathetic to just war theory, that pacifism was an attempt to *interpret* and apply the meaning of Christian love, not simply a clear commandment of the Gospels. As Bainton put it:

The rejection of military service on the part of the early church was not however derived from any explicit prohibition in the New Testament. The attitude of the Gospels to the soldiers' calling was neutral. The centurion was commended for his faith rather than for his profession, but was not called upon to abandon his profession (1960: 53).

Pacifism is an interpretation of the implications of the Christian faith and of Christian love. It was the stance of the earliest Christians. It has always been the stance of some Christians. But it did not remain the stance of most Christians or of most Christian churches or organizations. By A.D. 177 Christians fought as soldiers under the Stoic Marcus Aurelius in the provinces along the Danube (Ramsey 1961: xvi). But the decisive change occurred when Constantine converted to Christianity. Before then, Christians did not have political responsibility. They were ruled; they did not have the responsibility of rule. They had been enjoined to "render unto Caesar what is Caesar's," an ambiguous teaching perhaps, but they had never had the burden of being Caesar, with the responsibilities that may entail for protecting peace and good order or for restraining humans burdened with a fallen nature. In assuming the burdens of rule, Christians abandoned pacifism. Some Christians have thought that a fall, a betrayal. Most have not. They thought, instead, that (the words are Ramsey's):

The change-over to just war doctrine and practice was not a "fall" from the original purity of Christian ethics; but, however striking a turning-full-circle, this was a change of tactics only. The basic strategy remained the same: responsible love and service of one's neighbor in the texture of the common life. . . . Christians simply came to see that the service of the real needs of all the men for whom Christ died required more than personal, witnessing action. It also required them to be involved in maintaining the organized social and political life in which all men live (1961: xvii).

To illustrate (utilizing one of the horrors of this age), when the Nazis come for oneself, nonresistance may be an expression of love. When they come for one's Jewish or Gypsy neighbor, it is not so clear that Christian nonresistance is an expression of love. That the developing doctrine of just war was in fact a serious attempt to apply the love ethic of Christ, and not merely a weakening of faith or a cowardly inability to face the sacrifices of nonresistance, is demonstrated by the fact that the earliest versions of the doctrine allowed the use of armed forces for police and military duties—to preserve order and justice, to preserve the community and protect one's neighbor, to protect the innocent from the guilty—but did not allow personal self-defense. The Christian would fight to defend his neighbor, or his community, but not to defend his own life against violent attack (Ramsey

1961: xvii–xviii; Bainton 1960: 97–8). The object of just war was to "vindicate justice and restore peace"; the "motive must be love" (Bainton 1960: 14). Just war theory, like pacifism, was an interpretation of what love required. And, as Christians assumed the responsibilities of rule in the world, just war theory became and remained for many centuries the dominant Christian interpretation of what Christian love requires, an interpretation only vigorously challenged again in the recent past.

The third tradition with regard to war and peace in the Christian community is the tradition of the crusade, or holy war. The distinction between the just war and the crusade is summed up by George Weigel (1987a: 38; cf. Weigel 1987b: 38–41):

In the crusade tradition, war is a positive moral good: it expresses the will of God in the world; it punishes the heathen, whoever they are; it cleanses the world of sin; and it advances the claims of the Gospel. The just war tradition, which is a *minimalist* tradition, views war as a moral tragedy: one that may be unavoidable in certain circumstances, but a moral tragedy nonetheless. War, according to just war theorists, is never a positive good; it can be the lesser of evils, one which has the ultimate intention of restoring community with the adversary.

The three traditions—pacifism, just war, and the crusade—are not, according to Bainton, based on different views of God or of fallen human nature. The question, instead, is how to deal with human depravity and the relationship of the church and the world. And Bainton gives a clear summary of the traditional relationships of the three traditions to the world:

Pacifism has commonly despaired of the world and dissociated itself either from society altogether, or from political life, and especially from war. The advocates of the just war theory have taken the position that evil can be restrained by the coercive power of the state. The Church should support the state in this endeavor and individual Christians as citizens should fight under the auspices of the state. The crusade belongs to a theocratic view that the Church, even though it be a minority, should impose its will upon a recalcitrant world. Pacifism is thus often associated with withdrawal, the just war with qualified participation, and the crusade with dominance of the Church over the world (1960: 14–15).

Bainton's is a fair summary of the traditional understanding. But in this century there has been, among many, a fundamental alteration in the stance of pacifism and pacifists, or pacifist organizations, toward the world.

THE SPREAD OF A NEW, HYBRID PACIFISM

Christian pacifism has traditionally been the province of those who withdraw from the struggles of the world. It was restricted, in Roman Catholicism, to those who withdrew to the monasteries, or who followed certain of the religious vocations—priests and monks were not ordinarily allowed to serve in the military, but the laity were. It was restricted, in Protestantism, mainly to sects that withdrew completely or, as in the case of the Society of Friends in early America, to sects that participated in politics, but not in votes on such measures as raising military forces. Quakers, that is, would not themselves participate in war or in raising military forces, but they would not try to compel their pacifism upon their neighbors against their neighbors' consciences. Traditionally, then, to be a pacifist or a member of the traditional peace churches was to withdraw, at least in part, from the world. But that changed greatly in this century, even as pacifism spread broadly beyond the traditional peace churches into the mainline Protestant denominations, both here and in certain of the other democracies, such as Great Britain. Indeed, the most notable characteristic of the new pacifism was its commitment to be effective in the world. It meant not only to give witness to peace, but also to give a lead in actually establishing peace in the world. It is worth looking, then, at both the spread of pacifism beyond its traditional homes in the monasteries and the peace churches and at the efficacy of the measures advocated by the new pacifists in their pursuit of peace.

The spread of pacifism among the churches and within religious organizations between the World Wars was both rapid and extensive. This was, in part, a reaction to what many saw, after the event, as too uncritical support for the Allies during the last war. Looking back, it seemed that the Allies were not, after all, so virtuous, that their sordid motives had been revealed by the scramble for gain at the peace table, that naive church people had been manipulated by clever but unprincipled war propaganda, and that, worst of all, the church people and the churches had all too readily given up their scruples about war in order to sanctify an unholy slaughter as a holy crusade. (Ray Abrams' very influential 1933 study, *Preachers Present Arms*, provided the definitive expression of this view.)

The new pacifism was born, as well, of the conviction, derived from the horrors of World War I, with its massed artillery barrages, its mass charges into machine gun fire, and its deadly use of planes, tanks and poison gas, that modern, technological mass war was simply too terrible, its slaughter disproportionate to any rational end, and that it was, consequently, immoral and unthinkable under any circumstances. Just war theory was discredited because, in this view, the horrors of modern war could not be brought within its terms. But perhaps it was more than that. Donald Meyer, assessing the new pacifist stance, said that for the pacifist and neutralist churchmen, their divisions were always reconciled by their agreement that "war gained nothing, war was worse than anything, always" (1960: 353).

There were changes, too, in the understanding of the locus of evil, of the potential for establishing the Kingdom in this world, and of the possibilities for peace. At the least, one can say that these Christians hoped for more than Christians had hoped for, in this world, for many centuries.

The turn to pacifism among a number of mainline churches was led by those who met in a number of umbrella operations, most notably the Fellowship of Reconciliation (FOR), and it was spurred by the backing of influential journals such as *Christian Century* and *The World Tomorrow*. The rapidity and extent of that turn is suggested by the results of a number of polls, admittedly nonscientific, initiated by Kirby Page. The first, conducted by *The World Tomorrow* in 1931, was sent to about 53,000 ministers, of whom some 19,372 responded. The results, from the point of view of traditional just war theory, were startling: 62 percent of those replying believed that the churches should go on record as "refusing to sanction or support any future war" (Chatfield 1971: 127–28). While this poll was not sent to Jews, Roman Catholics, Lutherans, Southern Baptists, or Southern Methodists, it did reveal that more than 12,000 ministers had come to believe that their churches should refuse to sanction any war, and that pacifism had clearly broken the bounds of the traditional peace churches.

In 1934 the poll was repeated. This time, 67 percent of the more than 20,000 who replied would have the churches refuse to sanction any future war (Ibid.: 128). Moreover, there was additional advice—82 percent opposed military training in high schools and colleges, 77 percent wanted reduced armaments in the United States, "regardless of the action of other countries," and only 36 percent "regarded the distinction between 'defensive' and 'aggressive' war as sufficiently clear to justify their participation in a so-called war of defense" (Van Kirk 1934: 7).

Parallel results were obtained by James Baker, a Methodist bishop, two years later. This was after the Reichstag fire. This was after Hitler had seized power and made himself Führer. This was after Hitler had repudiated the treaty of Versailles, invoked anti-Semitic laws, and led Germany into open and furious rearming in violation of treaties. This was after Mussolini, having stared down the League of Nations, invaded Abyssinia (Ethiopia). This was during the year in which Hitler led Germany into the Rhineland and Spain dissolved into a civil war backed, on the one side, by Nazi Germany and, on the other, by the Soviet Union. This was the year, indeed, when the fascist powers, led by Hitler and Mussolini, formed their Axis. Yet 56 percent of the 13,000 ministers who responded to Baker's poll still were able to say that they would refuse to sanction any future war (Meyer 1960:

354). Whatever the exact meaning of these polls, the results are an indication that pacifism had become, at the least, a significant position among ministers of mainline Protestant churches.

In truth, if Robert Miller is correct, pacifism had become more than that, it had become, even by the early 1920s, the " 'party line' of liberal Protestantism" (Miller 1971: 403). John C. Bennett, speaking of the whole period between World War I and World War II, observed that "in many Christian circles between the wars 'the burden of proof . . . shifted to the non-pacifist' " (Meyer 1960: 330). And Walter Van Kirk, Secretary of the Department of International Justice and Good Will of the Federal Council of Churches, after compiling all the official pronouncements, resolutions and proclamations made by Protestant churches and religious peace groups during the 1920s and early 1930s, was able to proclaim that, in the title of his 1934 book, *Religion Renounces War*. Certainly there was evidence. Van Kirk documented resolutions to that effect from an extraordinary number of general conventions and official church statements (See Van Kirk 1934, "Parting Company with Caesar," 1–45). In addition, Van Kirk was able to report that "When the Federal Council of Churches, in 1932, declared that the church as an institution should neither sanction nor bless war, there were only one or two dissenting voices among the four hundred delegates representative of the twenty-five communions adhering to the council" (1934: 44).

In view of the evidence, it is fair to say that for many church leaders between World Wars I and II, and for many Protestant church organizations, if not for their laity, Christianity entailed pacifism, the refusal to sanction or participate in any war. Even as late as February 1941, after France and much of Europe had fallen to the furious German onslaught, and British forces had been driven from the continent, some of this sentiment remained. Bainton reports that:

The Episcopalians were ready to support Britain; the Presbyterians were of divided counsels; the Disciples were noninterventionist; while the Methodists and the Congregationalists still reflected the strong pacifist sentiment of the previous decade. Curiously, while the other Protestant churches were veering toward war the Lutherans were detaching themselves from their traditional adherence to the doctrine of the just war. As for Catholics, a poll of 54,000 students disclosed 97 percent opposed to our entry into the conflict (1960: 219).

ASSUMPTIONS AND STRATEGIES

The strong movement away from just war theory and toward pacifism among Protestant church leaders and organizations between the wars was not a movement away from engagement in the world. Quite the contrary, this new pacifism was characterized by the attempt to mobilize opinion and influence government policies. That is, the new pacifism was characterized, not by the traditional withdrawal from the world, but by energetic attempts to act in the world so as to bring about an end to war. This was an engaged pacifism. It is appropriate, then, to examine the policies these pacifists preferred, and assess their impacts. One question is whether the new politically engaged pacifism effectively broke out of the older Christian understanding that pacifism, in a world of fallen men, can only be a way for the few seeking perfection, or for a sect that withdraws, but not a way to live in the world with political responsibility. Let us look, then, at pacifist strategies to secure peace between the wars.

How was war to be avoided? Donald Meyer, assessing pacifist strategies, said that for these church people: " . . . the way to eliminate war was to support every policy consistent with absolute peace, oppose every policy and measure that accepted even the possibility of war" (1960: 352). That overstates the case somewhat, no doubt. But it is best to be specific. For that, let us examine policies advocated by two of the leaders of the church peace movement, Kirby Page and Charles Morrison. Page, who served for a time as Secretary of the FOR and was Chief Editor from 1926 to 1934 of *The World Tomorrow*, was for "American membership in League and World Court, American support for the outlawing of war, abandonment of all military and political imperialism in Latin America and Asia, freedom for the

Philippines, reduction and if necessary cancellation of war debts both Allied and German, reduction of tariffs, disarmament led by America" (Meyer 1960: 155). His support for the League was qualified, typically, by "reservations against the League's power to apply sanctions" (Ibid.: 352). Sanctions, it must be remembered, could lead to war. Charles Chatfield, in summing up Page's policies, describes him as a leader in the "antipreparedness cause" (1971: 146).

Charles Morrison, like Kirby Page, was a leader in the peace movement, and a political pacifist. He was editor of the *Christian Century*, the leading journalistic voice of liberal Protestantism by the middle 1930s. He was a leader in the battle for the Kellogg Peace Pact of 1928, which outlawed aggressive war (Meyer 1960: 53). Under his guidance, the *Christian Century* fought conscription, rearmament, the destroyers-for-bases deal, lend-lease, entanglement with Britain or France, aid to Britain, any breach of neutrality. He was for negotiated settlements of differences, and led the fight to adopt the Van Zeeland proposals for economic rearrangements in Europe. He was instrumental in getting first the Federal Council of Churches and then, under its pressure, the World Council of Churches to agree to some type of international meeting to try to arrange, through some concessions, a negotiated settlement. In the end, as Meyer puts it: "Thirty-four persons, therefore, collected in the Europe of July, 1939, to discuss reallocation of the world" (1960: 373). Meyer adds that the 34 produced a statement, which the *Christian Century* then published, but by then war had broken out. In the same vein, Morrison proposed in May 1940 that President Roosevelt send a delegation to all the neutral capitals in Europe to assemble a peace conference to devise a radically new Europe. The idea was picked up and discussed. Unfortunately, by then there were, as Meyer notes, "fewer neutral capitals . . . " (1960: 373).

Page and Morrison, FOR, the *Christian Century* and *The World Tomorrow*, the Federal Council of Churches, many individual church organizations, and the religious peace movement intended to be effective. They put pressure on political leaders and the government. They hoped to secure peace by fostering policies of participation in international organizations (the League), by outlawing war (the Kellogg pact), by agreements to settle conflicts without war (the Locarno pact of 1925 and others), by disarming either unilaterally (opposition to the 1927 naval cruiser programs and subsequent arms programs) or by agreements to limit arms (the Washington and London conferences), and by finding just economic settlements that would resolve what were thought to be the economic causes of war (opposition to imperialism, Japanese exclusion and, on the positive side, changes of trade policy, forgiveness of debts, etc.), and by insistence on noninvolvement and neutrality. Some of this was sound, as far as it went. But it did not go very far. Consider.

The religious peace movement was, in principle, internationalist. It supported the League of Nations. That support was vitiated, however, by a fatal flaw. While the movement supported international condemnation of aggression, it tended to oppose all sanctions, for sanctions might lead to war. In the case of Italy, for example, the League threatened sanctions if Mussolini invaded Abyssinia. Mussolini warned, in return, that he would not tolerate any sanctions that would hinder his invasion. The League members, fearful that sanctions might involve them in war, then *deliberately imposed non-effective sanctions*. Winston Churchill pointed to the absurdity of this. Under pacifist restrictions— sanctions must not lead to war—the League "proceeded to the rescue of Abyssinia on the basis that nothing must be done to hamper the invading Italian armies" (Churchill 1948: 176).

This was not a good beginning for the new engaged, presumably effective, pacifism. As Reinhold Niebuhr put it: "Is it really 'Christian,' is it God's will, never to call the bluff of a bully for fear that you might be involved in violence? Then we had better prepare for the complete victory of the barbarism that is spreading over Europe" (Robertson 1976: 170–71). And in fact the Abyssinian conquest illustrates the traditional failing of an engaged, political pacifism. If one is interested in achieving a degree of justice and order in the world, then one must be willing, if necessary, to resist armed aggression with violence. Collective condemnation of Mussolini's aggression came to nothing because it lacked that willingness. Lacking that, the League, when pushed, sacrificed the Abyssinian neighbor.

Support for the League without support for the sanctions necessary to make the League meaningful was characteristic of the new pacifism and the peace movement that dominated the democracies between the wars. The Kellogg-Briand Peace Pact, for example, which outlawed aggressive war, was hailed by many with enormous enthusiasm. Morrison and Page had campaigned hard for it. Frank Kellogg, the United States Secretary of State, proclaimed that "we have made peace at last." Aristide Briand, the French Foreign Minister, believed that this "marked a new day in the history of mankind." Nearly everyone signed. Still, and characteristically, the treaty lacked enforcement provisions. As the historian Barbara Tuchman dryly noted: "In short, it was empty" (1982: 93).

Equally enthusiastically supported, hailed with enormous enthusiasm, were the Locarno Treaties of 1925. By these treaties, designed to bind nations by solemn commitment to settle matters peacefully, Germany bound itself to "pursue the course of arbitration in any disputes with Belgium, France, Poland or Czechoslovakia" (Tuchman 1982: 93). One's euphoria is tempered, however, by notice that each nation bound to Germany in this agreement—Belgium, France, Poland, and Czechoslovakia—was soon betrayed, and conquered, by Germany.

The new pacifism was not wrong to try to establish commitments to the peaceful settlement of disputes, but there still must, finally, be the will and the force to enforce such commitments. That, indeed, was the burden of Churchill's observation: "No foreign policy can have validity if there is no adequate force behind it and no national readiness to make the necessary sacrifices to produce that force" (1948: 376–77). Unfortunately, neither the peace movements in the democracies nor the religious peace movement in the United States displayed the will, or supported creation of the necessary military strength, to enforce the treaties, such as Locarno and Kellogg, that they so fervently grasped. They depended, instead, entirely upon the good will and good faith of the other side. There came a day when that good will and faith were not there.

There was, in fact, a touching faith in the power of the promise by those who hoped for peace. There was an avid quest for signatures on pieces of paper. The dictators were happy to oblige. The promises were then violated, when it suited the dictators. But this only produced a constant search for new agreements, new promises. And again, the dictators were happy to oblige. At one point Churchill had occasion to remark upon this credulity:

The Prime Minister has confidence in the good will and in the word of Herr Hitler, although, when Herr Hitler broke the Treaty of Versailles, he undertook to keep the Treaty of Locarno, and when he broke the Treaty of Locarno, he undertook not to interfere further, or to have further territorial claims in Europe. When he entered Austria by force, he authorized his henchmen to give an authoritative assurance that he would not interfere with Czechoslovakia. That was less than six months ago. Still the Prime Minister believes that he can rely upon the good faith of Hitler (1948: 325–26).

This speech was made to the House of Commons just after Neville Chamberlain had returned from Munich announcing, to a euphoric public, that: "This is the second time there has come back from Germany to Downing Street peace with honor. I believe it is peace in our time" (cited in Churchill 1948: 318). But this promise, too, produced neither peace nor honor. Nor was there much excuse for this naivete on the part of those committed to peace. History is replete with examples of broken promises between nations. One need look no further back than World War I, when Germany dismissed its violation of the pledge to honor Belgium's neutrality as merely the violation of " '*ein Fetzen Papier*' ('a scrap of paper')" (Manchester 1988: 63). Securing promises from dictators, without the will or the power to enforce them, a characteristic of the new pacifism and of the pacifistic democracies between the wars, did not prove a fruitful path to peace.

But perhaps arms themselves were the problem. Kirby Page had argued that by "aggressive good will" before World War I Germany's neighbors could have shown Germany that no harm was intended them, and that the German public, relieved of its fears, would have removed the German militarists from power, thereby securing peace (Meyer 1960: 157). The implication was that nations arm from fear, and that by unilateral reduction or elimination of arms, fear would be removed, thus producing peace. But neither history nor the thirties served this theory well. There are, no doubt, wars fought out of fear. But there are wars fought as well for revenge, for domination, for gain and glory, or pride and honor, or to serve a master race or the purposes of the proletariat in history, or for empire and dominion. And disarmament in the face of a nation that seeks, for example, revenge may not be a path to peace. Certainly reduction of arms in the face of the dictators of the 1930s did not lead to peace.

Closely related to the idea that arms themselves are the problem was the notion that the democracies should refuse to engage in an arms race because arms races "always lead to war." Thus pacifists, here and abroad, fiercely resisted engaging in an arms race with the dictators. It is enlightening to examine the record of the great political parties in Great Britain on this point. There the Labor Party was led for years between the wars by George Lansbury, a Christian saint according to Reinhold Niebuhr (Robertson 1976: 167), and a pacifist (Churchill 1948: 67). It was led again by Ramsey MacDonald, Prime Minister in a coalition government, and all his life a pacificist (Manchester 1988: 77). MacDonald, true to his faith, was proud of having rapidly dismantled England's armed forces (Ibid.: 95), and he was thoroughly opposed to rearmament, to sanctions that might lead to war, and to collective security that might require intervention on behalf of allies. Clement Attlee, a third Labor Party leader, was an equally strong proponent of pacifism and disarmament (Ibid.: 87).

Under such leadership, the Labor Party, arm in arm with the Liberal Party, steadfastly resisted all attempts at military preparedness. Thus, in 1934, the Labor and Liberal parties, in the face of Germany's rapid rearming in violation of treaties, opposed more money for arms on grounds, respectively, that it would jeopardize disarmament and that arms races always lead to war (Churchill 1948: 114). The British Labor and Liberal parties continued down this line to the very brink of disaster, always campaigning against "Tory armaments." Indeed, in 1935 the Labor and Liberal parties opposed *any* arms appropriations (Manchester 1988: 142). In December 1936, Labor still opposed rearmament (Ibid.: 220), and even in April 1939, both parties still opposed conscription (Churchill 1948: 355–56). The Conservative Party was only slightly better. All sides marched down this road of folly. In America, religious pacifists also took this road, believing that armaments, and arms races, lead to war. They worked vigorously to remove this nation from the race. Still, the refusal to race, while one's deadly enemies raced on, was an ill-conceived strategy. It cost dearly when the race was over, and the enemy had won.

Another fervently held notion was that a major cause of war was the desire for profits by the munitions makers. Acting on this assumption, one of the great rallying cries of the peace movement became: "Take the profits out of war!" Munitions makers were scorned as "Merchants of Death." Wars, of course, had long predated capitalism. No matter. Under the impact of the peace movement, attempts were made, here and in other democracies, to remove the profits from the arms industry. In the United States, the Senate, following the Nye committee hearings (which caused a national sensation according to Charles DeBenedetti 1980: 126), ratified an international convention designed to reduce the arms trade (Chatfield 1971: 164–67). And it is true that the German war industries made great profits. But it did not profit the democracies to refuse to match them in arms for fear of giving blood money to industrialists. But by the time this was recognized, it was too late, and most of the democracies of Europe had been conquered, and a nearly disarmed Britain struggled on, alone, saved only by the channel, and by those few, very few, airmen fighting enormous odds.

Regarding arms as the problem, in the face of rapidly arming dictators with grandiose plans of conquest, proved to be folly. But the new pacifism had three arrows left in its quiver. The first was arms limitation by agreement. Arms limitation agreements were in fact sought with fervor, and greeted with applause. Each was regarded as a step toward peace. One of the most famous of these was the Washington Naval Conference of 1922, which succeeded in limiting battleships of the United States, Britain, and Japan in the ratio of 5–5–3. This was regarded as a great victory for peace. Tuchman notes, however, that "Because Japan furiously resented holding the short end of the 5–5–3 ratio, the effect of the treaties was ultimately negative" (1982: 93). The Washington Naval Conference was followed by the London Conference of 1930, which put some limits on naval tonnages and on submarines, "amiably softened," reports Tuchman, "by an escalator clause which allowed an increase over specified tonnage if the 'national needs' of any signatory demanded it" (1982: 93).

Winston Churchill, who had to lead Britain in a deadly war against terrible odds, has made some pungent comments upon the effects of these arms limitation treaties, plus some others. The effect of the Anglo-American treaty of 1935 was, in his words, to allow "Germany a Programme of new construction which would set her yards to work for at least ten years. There was, therefore, no practical limitation or restraint of any kind imposed upon German naval expansion" (1948: 138). The general effect of these treaties was, he observed, to allow Germany to build much larger battleships (they cheated on the Treaty of Versailles and were not a party to later treaties that limited size); to allow both Germany and Japan to build for years as furiously as they could without worrying the democracies (they were allowed to buy the treaties); and to allow Germany the additional advantages that accrued to those who cheat—it ignored important treaty limitations. As Churchill put it, furiously, in 1936: "Once again we alone are injured by treaties" (1948: 13–14, 137–142, 160–61, 163, 464).

When war came, it was Churchill who was in the best situation to assess the impact of the arms limitation treaties. Treaties, he noticed, bound those who do not cheat. His deadly enemies cheated. Treaties enabled his enemies to build furiously, for years, without alarming those they intended to conquer, because the proposed victims had agreed to the treaties as a step to peace. Treaties also failed to seriously limit the important ships of World War II, aircraft carriers and submarines, while limiting, if ineffectively, the important ships of the last war, battleships. And in fact, if the dictators intended war, as they did, then an arms limitation treaty was something to negotiate to one's advantage, or to cheat upon, or to adhere to while transferring those resources to some other area that would confer advantage. If one is limited in battleships, build aircraft carriers; if limited in tonnages, build bombers. In the absence of serious peaceful intent on both sides, arms limitations were in fact likely to work to the advantage of those who intended war.

But the problem with arms limitation treaties is deeper. The strategy of arms limitation treaties grasps the problem at the wrong end. "It is the greatest mistake to mix up disarmament with peace. When you have peace you will have disarmament" (Churchill 1948: 102). It is ill will that leads to armaments. "Europe will be secure when nations no longer feel themselves in great danger, as many of them do now. Then the pressure and the burden of armaments will fall away automatically . . . and it might be quite easy to seal a movement of that character by some general agreement" (Ibid.: 102). Churchill was backed in his estimate by the Chairman of the League of Nations Disarmament Commission, Salvador de Madariaga. Assessing his long experience, he concluded: "The trouble with disarmament is that the problem of war is tackled upside down and at the wrong end . . . . Nations don't distrust each other because they are armed; they are armed because they distrust each other. And therefore to want disarmament before a minimum of common agreement on fundamentals is as absurd as to want people to go undressed in winter" (Tuchman 1982: 98). In actual fact, the arms limitation treaties did not prevent the dictators from building furiously in preparation for their conquests. The dictators gained initial superiority, and used it to devastating effect. And finally, of course, if one really is pacifist, what is one to do when cheating is proved, or invasion comes? The pacifists, and the pacifistic democracies, again seriously underestimated the gravity of the situation, and proposed ineffective measures, while resisting those measures that might have cowed, and deterred, their enemies.

Two additional strategies recommended themselves to the new pacifists. One was the attempt to avoid war by eliminating the injustices leading to war, and special emphasis was placed upon the economic injustices. Morrison, of the *Christian Century*, for example, was a zealous advocate of the economic rearrangements for Europe proposed by the Belgian statesman, Paul Van Zeeland. Morrison pushed for a meeting of churchmen, and got it to discuss, as Meyer puts it, "Reallocation of the world" (1960: 373). But it was hard to see how this was supposed to help. If it were wrong of Britain to colonize India (as these churchmen thought), then how could it be right to obtain peace by making sure that Germany, too, gained the illicit spoils of a colonial empire? The moral logic involved here is a bit murky. Moreover, is the world to be redivided each time an excluded power is denied a share? Is that not an invitation to become a power, and then make demands? And what if there is no agreement on what the allocation is to be? What, in fact, would have satisfied Hitler, or the Japanese? Was what Hitler wanted just? Was it possible to give? If those who were to give refused, then what? It was a muddle, not the least a moral muddle. And, as the Allies were to discover, each appeasement of the appetite of Hitler merely whetted his appetite for more, and caused him to respect, and fear them, the less. This was not an effective strategy for peace.

Finally, the pacifists, and the peace movement in the United States, tried to achieve peace, if not for others, at least for this nation, by seeking to avoid entanglement, by seeking to avoid taking sides. The pacifists ended, in effect, as allies of the isolationists, the America Firsters, the Fortress America crowd. It was an odd alliance. And it did not work. Neutrality was sought. And it did work for some. It worked for Sweden and Switzerland. Sweden, which supplied much of the iron ore for the Nazi war machine, managed to remain neutral while nations all around it were conquered and occupied. The same was true of Switzerland. But the attempt to stay neutral did not work for Holland, or Belgium, or Denmark, or Norway. It did not work, in the end, for the United States. Staying out of war depends, finally, upon others, and whether they wish to war on you. The attempt to remain neutral by Holland and Belgium failed, if for no other reason, because Germany found the best way to conquer France was to come through these two nations. The attempt by the United States failed when Japan bombed Pearl Harbor and Hitler, who scorned what he thought a flabby democracy, declared war the next day. The pacifist and American desire to stay neutral failed because our enemies disregarded it.

But there is an additional point that should be made. Christian pacifism has viewed itself as the proper expression of Christian love, but it is hard to see how watching one country after another be conquered by fascist dictators without doing anything to help— while standing aside in neutrality—was an expression of love. This indeed was Neibuhr's charge—that to be neutral in such a contest was a loveless choice that sacrificed the innocent neighbor (Meyer 1960: 396–97). This was, in fact, the criticism that Dean Shailer Mathews of the Divinity School of the University of Chicago had made of Kirby Page's pacifism in 1918. It was, he said, "as if the Good Samaritan, if he had come down a little earlier, had waited until the robbers had finished with the traveler before he assisted him" (Chatfield 1971: 45–46).

WHY THE NEW, HYBRID PACIFISM FAILS

The period between the World Wars was marked by a great shift of religious opinion, a shift spearheaded by certain interdenominational organizations, such as the FOR and the journals *The World*

Tomorrow and *Christian Century*. It took new developments in theology, especially the Social Gospel movement, and new attitudes toward what was possible and necessary, and a revulsion against the horrors revealed by World War I, and produced a new type of pacifism, a pacifism that was politically engaged in the world, a pacifism that intended to influence the policies of governments in such a way that those governments would effectively avoid or prevent war. This was new. In the past pacifists, in the main, had withdrawn from this sinful world. They had not expected wars to cease, nor to influence the powers of this world. They stood, instead, in their monasteries, or sects, as a reproach to this world and a testimony in favor of the next. They refused the things that were Caesar's. The older pacifism, in rejecting political power, rejected political responsibility, or left it to others acting according to different standards.

The traditional alternative to pacifism or withdrawal was just war theory. Those who accepted political responsibility in the world—and most Christians over the whole span from the time of Constantine until the present have accepted such responsibility as a duty of Christian love—accepted, as well, a responsibility to use force if necessary, precisely as a necessary deduction of what Christian love requires of those with political responsibility if the neighbor is to be protected. The use of Caesar's power was legitimate because we are our brother's keeper, and in this world to accept that responsibility is to accept the necessity of the use of force.

The new pacifism, which spread broadly among the mainline Protestant churches between the wars, was a hybrid. It accepted from traditional pacifism the refusal to accept violence or engage in war. It accepted from traditional just war theory the appropriateness of acting in the world, accepting political power, and using it for the goal of peace, and of protection of the neighbor. The question that is posed is whether such a hybrid makes sense. Can one be fully committed to peace under all circumstances and also be committed to effective action in the world to protect the innocent neighbor? Why had the church, when it accepted political responsibility, also given up pacifism?

The experience between the wars gives strong support to the traditional positions of pacifism and just war, and very little support for the new hybrid. The engaged hybrid pacifism of the interwar period (along with the larger peace movement) was quite effective in influencing the policies of the great democracies, especially those of Great Britain and the United States. And those great pacifistic democracies failed to deter war. Indeed, most of the democracies of Europe were conquered. But what, in particular, was wrong with the hybrid? The answer is that it sacrifices the innocent and disarms those who would resist evil. Consider.

The new pacifism remained pacifism. It refused to fight. But that refusal undermined the effectiveness of nearly every policy it supported in the pursuit of peace. The new engaged pacifism supported international organization for peace. It supported the League of Nations and the World Court. But it had a reservation. It *was* pacifist. It would not support war. It would not support sanctions that might lead to war. It supported verbal condemnation of aggressors, or even sanctions if those sanctions would not bother the aggressors so much that the aggressors might fight over them. It condemned Italy for its designs on Abyssinia, but it did nothing to stop Mussolini when he set about to conquer Abyssinia. It accepted responsibility for the neighbor in the world, but when the dictator chose to conquer the neighbor, it sacrificed the neighbor rather than fight the dictator. This was neither effective nor an obvious expression of love for the Abyssinian neighbor. The new pacifism was fervently for peace and justice. But when the dictator's armies marched, it was for peace—its own peace—not for justice, and not for the Abyssinians, who got neither peace nor justice. And that was the problem, again and again. The new pacifism, then, could organize international organizations endlessly. But all that effort, all that organization and collective action, was made futile, absolutely bootless, by the refusal, if necessary, to use force to protect justice and the neighbor. What do dictators, after all, massing their tanks and bombers, care about verbal condemnations? In the event, we found out. Nothing.

The new pacifism also put much energy into seeking international treaties and promises—whether to settle disputes peacefully (Locarno), to limit weapons or disarm (the Washington and London Naval treaties), to outlaw aggressive war (the Kellogg-Briand Pact), to guarantee borders (the Locarno Pact again), or to secure promises that the dictators would not do something (or do it again, or again, or again). Some of this could have had merit, *had there been the will and the power to enforce these agreements and promises*. But the new pacifism was still pacifism. It shrank, in consequence, from using violence to enforce anything. And, unlike the traditional pacifism, it led the battle to ensure that its nonpacifist fellow citizens also were denied the military force levels they would have needed to enforce these treaties and promises. (One thinks of the British Liberal and Labor parties voting against *any* military appropriations in 1935 as Hitler's Germany furiously armed in preparation for war.) To what, indeed, was the new pacifism reduced? It was reduced to begging the dictators for promises that they would behave. And when the dictators did not, there was nothing left to do but beg them again. We saw, in due time, what Hitler thought of this.

As for deterrence, why this was the anti-preparedness cause. War was immoral. It should not be sanctioned. If one did not admit the morality of war, then one should not prepare for war. The pacifists opposed each effort to prepare in the face of dictatorial threats and aggressions. Indeed, the new pacifism proved extraordinarily susceptible to wishful thinking. The old pacifism knew that there was evil in the world and that the world was full of fallen men with evil designs on their neighbors. The new pacifism, which did not wish to admit the necessity of fighting to resist evil, or the necessity of resisting the designs of fallen men, kept seeking out theories that would enable it to have peace without the costs of building armies, or using them if deterrence failed. So the new pacifism was happy indeed to think that war could be stopped by the simple device of "taking the profits out of war," or refusing to engage in an arms race. So, too, the new pacifism was happy to believe that wars were mistakes, that if aggressive good will were shown, preferably by unilateral disarmament, why then other nations, realizing their own fears were groundless, would join in the disarmament, and the peace. So the new pacifists set out to reduce the dictators' fears. And they did. The dictators became quite fearless. But this did not produce what the pacifists hoped or expected. It helped produce, instead, the deaths of some fifty millions.

If one accepts the mantle of Caesar—the mantle of engagement in the world, or responsibility for enforcing a degree of harmony and order in the world, of protecting subjects and citizens—then love requires a realistic assessment of the proportions of things and a serious consideration of how fallen humans behave in this world and of what is necessary to restrain them from gratifying their worst desires. The engaged, hybrid pacifism between the wars failed those tests. It did not assess the full depth and gravity of the situation. It did not appreciate the full evilness of the intentions of its enemies. It did not take, or allow to be taken, the steps necessary to deter even the most monstrous evil. And it failed, not because of chance errors, but because, by its nature, the new political pacifism could not support what was needed.

The older understanding—an understanding that lasted many centuries—proved, in the light of the interwar period, to be correct. If one would be pacifist, then one must withdraw from the world, and leave to others the burden of being one's brother's keeper. Or, if one would take up the mantle of responsibility, of being one's brother's keeper, then one must lay down the commitment to pacifism, and assume the burden, at times, of using force, and engaging in war. What one cannot do is adopt the new hybrid, a politically engaged pacifism, because it fails, in the difficult cases, to do what is necessary to secure either peace or justice, and it fails, as well, to do what love requires for the innocent neighbor.

Let Winston Churchill, the democratic statesman who most clearly saw and warned of the errors of this movement, the statesman turned to by his desperately unprepared nation to lead it against some of history's most terrible foes when his unheeded warnings proved—as disaster piled on disaster—to be correct, render his judgment. The great peace movement possessed, he granted, "a sincere love of peace," but that was, he was compelled to add, "no excuse for muddling hundreds of millions of humble folk into total war" (1948: 190).[2]

Chapter 5

The Role of Religious Organizations in the Gay and Lesbian Rights Movement

Steven H. Haeberle

Religious institutions have not functioned as a source of leadership in the gay and lesbian rights movement in the United States. That is not to say that impetus for change is absent in the major American Christian and Jewish religious establishments. Rather, the level of movement activity within those groups reflects the pace of reform in the larger society. However, the role of religion is unique among social organizations in that some traditional religious teachings are perhaps singularly more responsible for why a "movement" has occurred at all.

At the midpoint of the twentieth century gay and lesbian Americans faced a system of prejudice in which legal, scientific, and religious institutions locked together in mutually reinforcing opprobrium. Legal and scientific views have changed through discourse based on secular liberal values and empirical research. Religious institutions, dependent on the interpretation of nonworldly phenomenon, have on the other hand proceeded with greater ambiguity.

Legal proscription on sexual activity was derived from religious dogma. The statutes of the American colonies cited scripture and "the mind of God" as reasons for punishing sex with the death penalty (Katz 1976: 31–37). As legal codes evolved, the deity was written out, often to be replaced by references to "unnatural acts," but the origin of the American concept of consensual sex as crime was clearly Christian.

The western liberal tradition, which values respect for the individual and a right of privacy, provided the underpinning for legal changes beginning in the 1960s when states began to decriminalize homosexual sex. Currently, 25 states and the District of Columbia still have "sodomy" laws pertaining to gays and lesbians on their books (Leonard 1989). Decriminalization represents removal of a restriction but not protection from social sanctions. Therefore, legal innovations have also included decisions to ban discrimination on the basis of sexual orientation in areas such as employment, housing, public accommodations, and credit. Interestingly, much more of this change has taken place in local government rather than at the national level. Nearly 70 municipalities and 16 counties provide some form of anti-discrimination protection to gays and lesbians (Leonard 1989). Only one state, Wisconsin, has a general law banning discrimination on the basis of sexual orientation. The national government has addressed the issue in civil service employment, but has not extended its coverage to private sector practices.

Science and medicine, too, have a rich history of homophobia in which clinical jargon served as a cover for religiously based ideas. Medical experts in the late nineteenth century began to define "sexual inverts" as a category of deviant persons. Katz (1976: 197–205) described the motives of these practitioners as having more to do with profit-making than morality. Nonetheless, religious teachings contributed to their stigmatization of gays and lesbians, and certainly played some role in the public explanations of their professional activity. For example, one Columbia University physician explained his treatment of homosexuals by stating, "it becomes my Christian manhood to act only as the vice-regent of the Almighty" (Dr. John D. Quackenbos quoted in Katz, 1976: 221). After several decades of applying "therapies," including castration, aversion therapy, and electroshock treatments, the medical establishment retreated from defining homosexuals as psychopathic personalities in 1973 (*New York Times* 1973).

The legal and medical histories are alike in two significant ways. First, the homophobia in both was motivated, at least in part, by a Christian view of morality. Second, each began to unravel for secular reasons. In the case of the sodomy statutes, countervailing liberal values of privacy and pluralism prevailed over puritan morality. In the case of the medical and psychological experts, overwhelming empirical evidence of normalcy among homosexuals toppled the theories of personality dysfunction. Put differently, whatever force religion may have had left by the 1970s as a rationale for homophobia in law and medicine, it had begun to lose to competing values.

Alternatively, homophobic religious institutions, by definition, are not bastions of competing secular values. Coping with anti-gay sentiments there necessitates confronting a more primal source of disapproval. To the extent that the gay and lesbian movement represents a broad-based effort to reform social organizations and practices, those activists who have worked in religious institutions have had a particularly arduous task of trying to repudiate a core set of values without benefit of equally compelling alternative mental frameworks within which to cast their arguments.

GAY AND LESBIAN ORGANIZATIONS IN THE RELIGIOUS COMMUNITY

The "Stonewall Riots" of June 1969 are conventionally taken as the symbolic beginning of the contemporary gay and lesbian rights movement. It marked the start of more widespread grass-roots participation in the movement, and was followed by an exponential increase in the number of gay and lesbian organizations across the 1970s. Gay and lesbian religious groups came into being during the same period when organizations were formed in most other institutional settings including business, the professions, labor, academe, and politics.

Most gay and lesbian religious organizations sprang up within established institutions. Generally, they share two sets of objectives. The first is internal. They provide support to their membership and attempt to affirm the religious validity of their sexual orientation. The second is external. They seek to assert an expanded, safer role for gays and lesbians within their own religious institution. Balancing these two goals is largely dependent on the level of homophobia within their religious reference groups.

The goals have a symbiotic relationship. The more homophobic the religious institution is, the more its gay and lesbian membership would be expected to need the services of a support group. Alternatively, religious organizations with lower levels of internal homophobia would give their gay and lesbian followers less reason to mobilize as a group. However, less homophobia also implies less resistance to organizing and greater acceptance of the demands of gay and lesbian groups. As a consequence, gay and lesbian organizations tend to be less visible in homophobic religious organizations and more active in those which are more hospitable to their presence.

Therefore, the institutional setting as well as the determination of religious gay and lesbian activists affect the scope and purpose of their agenda. At one end of the spectrum, supportive parent religious organizations such as the Unitarian-Universalist Association (UUA) and the Society of Friends are relatively accommodating to their gay and lesbian membership and have active organizations within the group. In contrast, gay and lesbian groups formed by adherents to more fundamentalist creeds such as Pentecostals and Evangelicals go virtually unrecognized, and occasionally deplored, by the hierarchy of their denominational groups. Goals and environment are thus bound together.

ORGANIZATION IN AN INCLUSIVE ENVIRONMENT

The development of gay and lesbian activities within the UUA and the Society of Friends moved along parallel tracks. Each had initial stirrings of awareness of sexual diversity in their congregations in the 1960s. Controversy began with the publication of *Toward a Quaker View of Sex* in 1963. It opened discussion on a variety of topics related to sex, including homosexuality. Although evangelical Quakers persisted in treating homosexuality as a "sin" from which people should repent, others in the denomination questioned the moral basis of anti-gay and lesbian attitudes in their belief systems (much of the information in this discussion comes from Grimes and Kaiser n.d.; North American FLGC 1988; Office of Lesbian and Gay Concerns 1990; and *Resolutions* n.d.).

That the realization of sexual diversity in these denominations came in the era of the civil rights movement undoubtedly served to heighten sensitivity to discrimination and bigotry directed toward lesbians and gay men. Many Unitarians and Quakers were active in the movement. The principles from which their opinions on racial equality emerged could provide a value structure for questioning homophobia.

Both the Quakers and Unitarians acted within a decade to recognize officially the position of gays and lesbians in their congregations. The Friends Committee for Lesbian and Gay Concerns (FLGC) dates from 1970. It was formed shortly after the *Friends Journal* published a pseudonymous story on what it was like to be gay and Quaker. The FLGC started meeting simultaneously with the Friends General Conference in 1972. Hooking onto the Quaker establishment in this way provided an impetus for action on two fronts. First, the contact with non-gay Friends motivated many of the latter to return to their own congregations with some understanding of the implications of homophobia. Consequently, a large number of Yearly Meetings passed resolutions between 1972 and 1974 calling for recognition of the civil rights of homosexuals. These included meetings held in Baltimore, Illinois, New York, the West Coast and Philadelphia. Thus, the action was not regionally centered. Second, gay and lesbian Friends also initiated greater organizational activity to create a network of local FLGC groups. Clearly, this represented a significant degree of organizational reform occurring within a relatively short time frame.

The experience of the UUA was similar. After some groundwork was laid in the 1960s, the denomination formally adopted a resolution in 1970 condemning discrimination against homosexuals and bisexuals in church affairs as well as in public life. It established an Office on Gay Affairs in 1973, which is now called the Office for Lesbian and Gay Concerns (OLGC). Its lay counterpart is Unitarian-Universalists for Lesbian and Gay Concerns (UULGC). It too has met annually during the UUA General Assembly, where interaction with non-gays has helped to stimulate reform within the group. Local churches and fellowships began to address the problems of homophobia, and the UULGC was able to create a national network of local chapters.

The timing of the activities in these two religious denominations was significant for its coincidence with secular social change. From the end of World War II to around 1970, the gay and lesbian rights movement in the United States had been an elite cause. It had attracted a small band of activists, who were dedicated to its goals, but it was clearly elite in the sense that the numbers of participants were limited (D'Emilio 1983; Adam 1987). Although the substantive significance of Stonewall may at times be overrated, it coincides with the transformation of the gay and lesbian rights movement from an elite-centered effort to a mass activity. That was the point in time when large numbers of gay and lesbian organizations sprang up in most urban areas as well as within other established associations and communities, and when the medical and legal professions began to question their attitudes about gays and lesbians.

It should not be surprising that gay and lesbian activity within religious organizations began simultaneously, nor should it have been unexpected for the beachhead of religious activity to have occurred within the Society of Friends and the UUA. Both are faiths which emphasize the importance of human experience. They seek to find meaning in life in a variety of ways. This frees them from adherence to a strict dogma or creed and allows for diversity among their followers. Each has been able to recognize gays and lesbians as part of their pluralistic religious constituency. This view was attained because of the primacy placed on the inherent worth of each individual. The human-centeredness of the theology makes it more amenable to evolution consistent with other trends in secular society as standards change.

However, having condemned discrimination and bigotry against gays and lesbians by the early 1970s, the Quakers and the UUA still had to confront a series of issues regarding the assimilation of sexual diversity in their ranks. These included gay and lesbian clergy, marriage, and the remnants of homophobia, often subtle, within their membership. In other words, it became clear that achieving sexual pluralism would require much more than issuing a few resolutions and declarations.

First, the call for full civil rights for gays and lesbians quickly focused attention on the practices of the religious bureaucracies themselves. This led the American Friends Service Committee to include gays in their 1978 Affirmative Action Statement. Nonetheless, the Friends are only loosely organized. Groups such as the Friends General Conference and the Friends United Meeting operate autonomously. In fact, the latter was embroiled in controversy in 1988 when it denied employment to a gay man because of his sexual orientation. Thus, full civil rights within the Society is not as of yet an attained goal.

The UUA has been on record opposing employment discrimination within the Association since 1980 when its General Assembly passed a resolution calling on its member churches, fellowships, and organizations to hire qualified openly gay, lesbian, and bisexual religious leaders. The UUA, too, is a nonhierarchical organization. Hiring decisions are left up to the discretion of constituent churches and fellowships. Individual openly gay and lesbian clergy feel they face some greater problems securing settlement than do heterosexuals or closeted gays and have attributed this to residual homophobia in the denomination. To a certain extent this was confirmed by a 1987 opinion survey of the UUA membership which revealed a small, but strident, reserve of homophobia persisting in the organization. Although well in the minority, they expressed opposition to hiring gay and lesbian ministers, and in somewhat greater numbers indicated uneasiness with the idea of hiring gay and lesbian persons to work in the religious education programs of their congregations. In short, the commitment to full civil rights remains a goal the organization is working toward, not today's reality.

Second, the question of how the church could legitimize erotic love between persons of the same sex as it did for heterosexuals quickly emerged as an issue high on the agenda of the gay and lesbian rights movement within religious organizations. "Marriage" is today at least as much a legal institution as it is a religious rite. Clergy willing to perform a same-sex marriage ceremony faced the problem of laws preventing it. The matter was addressed with some semantic gymnastics. The Friends Meeting in Seattle in 1981 offered a "celebration of commitment" to two women as a way of recognizing that their relationship was meaningful both to them and to the Meeting. The celebration of commitment has been performed in many different Meeting Houses, and more recently ceremonies for same-sex couples have been termed marriages although the significance remains religious, not legal.

The UUA conducts "services of union" as its version of a same-sex marriage. The General Assembly provided for the ceremony by resolution in 1984, and at the same time directed its Department of Ministerial and Congregational Services to disseminate printed material to ministers and lay persons to assist them in planning services for gay and lesbian couples. The material describes the intent of the service as:

- a public profession of love for the partner;
- a public vow of commitment to the welfare of the other;

- a wish for recognition of the seriousness of their love;
- the blessing of the church on that love;
- a striving for permanence, depth, and dignity in the relationship (Wheatly 1985).

The service itself resembles a wedding ceremony with the exchange of vows and rings and ends with a ministerial pronouncement along the lines, "By the authority vested in me as a Unitarian Universalist minister, I recognize you as being spiritually united." The couple then receives a "Certificate of Union." Thus the significance of the ceremony is wholly religious, not legal.

Third, institutional acceptance of gays and lesbians in the religious community has precipitated a need to review organizational practices for vestiges of homophobia, which are often subtle, but deeply imbedded in language and action. The UUA, for example, is presently implementing a "Welcoming Congregation Program." It is intended to ensure that inclusive language is used in all services and that gays, lesbians, and bisexuals are made to feel a part of the UUA. That the program was begun a full 20 years after the denomination formally declared its opposition to discrimination against homosexuals and bisexuals indicates the extent to which homophobia may be ingrained in attitude, language, and action in ways many who consider themselves socially liberal would not suspect. At the same time, the program signifies a serious institutional commitment to gays, lesbians, and bisexuals as a part of the larger organization.

While the major issues for the inclusive religious organizations have been gay and lesbian clergy, marriage, and the eradication of obdurate homophobia, a set of more subtle controversies may have been developing under the surface. Given that these organizations are more accepting of gays and lesbians than most other religious groups, they tend to draw some membership from people looking for a place where they are not made to feel unwelcome because of their sexuality. These individuals may bring with them some views on spirituality that are more dogmatic than what is usually found in their new religious home. This may set up tension between gays and lesbians who are "birthright" Unitarians or Quakers and those who became Unitarians or Quakers because they are gay or lesbian. The latter may be glad to have found a religious setting in which they are not condemned for their sexual orientation, but are less interested in exploring the meaning of life in a setting that emphasizes diversities in experience, knowledge, and understanding.

Other issues arise in organizational matters. The OLGC was established to deal with homophobia within the UUA. Some believe it should direct its efforts to the places where the problems seem the most intractable. In practice, much of its intra-denominational communication is with the UULGC which has chapters in churches which appear to be the most receptive to addressing the problems of discrimination with regard to gays and lesbians. Indeed, the strongest advocates for maintenance of the office are often associated with the UULGC rather than the congregations without gay and lesbian organizations, where presumably the OLGC has more work yet to do.

On balance, the experience of the UUA and the Society of Friends represents the course of the gay and lesbian rights movement in a religious setting that is relatively open. It shows that declarations deploring discrimination may set a tone for institutional change, but that serious reform is a slow process. It often must address subtle matters of deep-seated bias that are difficult to recognize and extremely resistant to modification. In that way, the pace of the gay and lesbian rights movement in these religious organizations parallels the rate of change in many secular institutions.

ORGANIZATION IN AN EXCLUSIVE ENVIRONMENT

At the other end of the spectrum from the UUA and Society of Friends are religious organizations where gays and lesbians, although explicitly unwelcome, have formed their own associations to function as support groups. This enables them to continue to profess their chosen faiths while at the same time receive assurance that those leaders of their religious movements who oppose them are misinformed or misguided. Examples of two such organizations include the National Gay Pentecostal Alliance (NGPA) and Evangelicals Concerned (EC). Both operate in hostile environments (much of the following discussion relies on Blair 1982; NGPA 1990).

The NGPA dates from 1980 and EC from 1982. Both are lay organizations dedicated to the service of gays and lesbians within their faiths. Organizationally, both have national and local operations. The NGPA is somewhat more hierarchical with the national organization having divided the country into districts, each headed by an ordained minister, who is called an elder. They form the Board of Elders which oversees the organization. Alternatively, EC is more a loose confederation of locally-initiated chapters.

The NGPA officially describes its purpose as establishing a "network of churches where all people, regardless of sexual orientation, may worship in Spirit and in Truth" (NGPA 1990). Similarly, EC describes itself as "a national ministry of evangelical Christians concerned about the misunderstandings of homosexuality among evangelicals and misunderstanding of the Gospel among homosexuals" (Blair 1982: 29). Hence, the formal responsibilities of the groups include both support of constituent membership as well as reform of the parent religious organization.

In practice, most of their efforts are internal rather than external. A presbyter of the NGPA stated bluntly that to his knowledge, "no non-gay Pentecostal denomination approves of the work we do," and that his organization spent relatively little time trying to "re-educate anti-gay heterosexual Christians." Instead, they try to reach "our own people with God's love and to undo the damage done to many of them by other churches" (W. Carey of NGPA 1990, personal communication). The same is true of EC which publishes a quarterly newsletter, the *Record*, refuting anti-gay stands of religious leaders and reporting briefly on gay and lesbian-related events in other faiths.

The inner-directedness of both organizations is explicable in terms of both the needs of their membership and the larger religious environment in which they operate. First, the degree of homophobia among most evangelicals and Pentecostals undoubtedly creates a psychological crisis for many gays and lesbians raised in these faiths. Organizations such as NGPA and EC can do much to resolve the cognitive dissonance likely to be found among these individuals and reassure them of their self-worth in a hostile environment. Second, the external homophobia precludes the presence of a receptive audience in the larger religious body. That is, the message that gay and lesbian organizations wish to spread simply falls on deaf ears. Issues such as ordination of gays and lesbians and creation of "ceremonies of union" are clearly well beyond the present agenda of these groups. Thus, the needs of the gays and lesbians in exclusive religious communities, together with the unwillingness of those communities to confront homophobia, impel such organizations to set their goals on the emotional support of their membership rather than on institutional reform.

ORGANIZATIONS IN THE MIDDLE

Most contemporary American religious institutions are somewhere between acceptance and rejection of gays and lesbians. Although it is difficult to generalize, the approach to gays and lesbians seems to be that nothing is inherently wrong with a same-sex sexual orientation, as a frame of mind. The uneasiness arises when questions turn to matters that actually involve having sex. Action is much more provocative than thought. The issues which draw the most attention tend to be ordination of gay and lesbian clergy and the recognition of gay and lesbian couples.

With ordination the operative phrase often seems to be "practicing homosexual." The experience of three Lutheran seminarians is illustrative. In January 1988, shortly after the merger of three

Lutheran denominations into the Evangelical Lutheran Church in America, three openly gay students at Pacific Lutheran Theological Seminary announced they wished to be considered as candidates for the ministry. Church officials asked if they were "practicing homosexuals." Two declined to answer the question. The third said, "no," but that he intended to date with the ultimate goal of settling into a monogamous relationship. The two who refused to comment were denied candidacies, and the third student was admitted. However, he was told he must inform his bishop if he ever enters a relationship. In the discussion one side perpetually referred to "practicing" sex while the other spoke of relationships (Perry 1988: 37).

The Episcopal Church allows ordination of celibate gay priests. The United Methodist Church is a bit more specific, denying ordination to what it calls "self-avowed, practicing homosexuals" (Harding 1988: 11). Reformed Jews in July 1990 began to allow the confirmation of gays as rabbis. The collective schizophrenia is perhaps summed up in the position of the Presbyterian Church U.S.A., which is on record calling for its membership to work to decriminalize consensual adult sexual activity and to pass laws forbidding discrimination on the basis of sexual orientation in employment, housing, and public accommodations, but at the same time it denies the ordination of any gay or lesbian person to either the ministry or a lay position of leadership such as deacon (Presbyterians for Lesbian/Gay Concerns 1985).

Virtually all of these denominations have organizations of gays and lesbians among their membership. Integrity, a group for gay and lesbian Episcopals; Affirmation, for Methodists; and Presbyterians for Gay and Lesbian Concerns are among the Christian organizations, and there is also the World Congress for Gay and Lesbian Jewish Organizations as well as a number of other gay and lesbian groups for Jews. In fact, the 1991 edition of the *Gayellow Pages* (1990: 31–32) lists 41 national gay and lesbian religious organizations and publications. Typically, the success of gay and lesbian religious groups accrues more at the local than the national level, which parallels change in the political arena. Dignity, the organization for Catholics, reports 110 chapters, most of which meet at churches where they are welcomed. Other churches, including New York's St. Patrick's Cathedral, have evicted Dignity chapters (Freiberg 3/15/88, 8/16/88). The attitudes of local congregants seem to have much more to do with the acceptance of gays and lesbians than does national policy.

A second recurrent issue concerns the recognition of gay and lesbian couples. Most organized religions in the United States have no ceremony to legitimize gay and lesbian relationships. The Diocese of Newark, New Jersey was the first Episcopal group to bless gay and lesbian unions (Freiberg 3/29/88). However, reports abound of individual congregations within other denominations and in all parts of the country quietly holding ceremonies of union for gay and lesbian couples. If done publicly they are likely to invite a disagreement with the hierarchy of the organization (See, for example, Harding 1990). Otherwise, they go on relatively unnoticed and uncounted.

Again, the difference seems to be in the attitudes of local congregations. The diffusion of decision-making centers within religious organizations appears to have left them fairly permeable to the contemporary gay and lesbian rights movement despite official policies to the contrary.

AN INDEPENDENT RELIGIOUS ORGANIZATION

The alternative to organizing within an established religious group is to go independent. That is the path followed by the Universal Fellowship of the Metropolitan Community Church (UFMCC). It began with the Metropolitan Community Church of Los Angeles in 1968 and held its first General Conference in 1970. Presently, the UFMCC has over 200 congregations nationwide and sits on the National Council of Churches. It is a Christian denomination which takes as a given that humans are sexual beings and that sex is to be enjoyed. Its membership is made up primarily of gays and lesbians (see *Universal Fellowship Today* 1987).

The central purpose of the UFMCC is to be a Christian church for gays and lesbians. Hence, it has had little internal controversy over issues such as ordination of gays and lesbians or ceremonies of union. They are inherently a part of the church structure. It has, however, experienced some intra-denominational disputes over the content of its services, which likely stems from the fact that its membership comes from individuals whose backgrounds are in a variety of traditions from Baptist to Catholic and are, therefore, accustomed to different types of programs. Nonetheless, its functions are similar to those of the gay and lesbian groups within other religious communities. The major difference here is that the external environment becomes a constituency of religious organizations.

The UFMCC is Christian in doctrine. It attempts to provide support against Christian homophobia to its membership who have been raised in a variety of faiths. In that sense, the UFMCC is a Christian "home" for those made to feel uncomfortable in other religious settings. For that reason, the UFMCC expends some effort refuting the Biblical bases of homophobia. Members drawn from the most exclusive of other Christian groups may need that reassurance more than others. Additionally, the UFMCC encourages its members to follow a course of social action. Gay and lesbian rights are at the head of the list for activities including marches, demonstrations, and sit-ins. Nonetheless, the denomination maintains a firm commitment to overcoming racism and sexism and took a strong position in favor of the nuclear freeze. In part, it appears that the experience of homophobic discrimination has made the UFMCC more aware of the problems of discrimination facing others.

Externally, the essential message of the UFMCC is that Biblical doctrines relating to homosexuality have been misinterpreted and that gays and lesbians should be accepted as other Christians. The outside environment encompasses both the hierarchy of other institutional faiths as well as population as a whole.

The advantages and disadvantages of independent organization are straightforward. The UFMCC can set its rules and agenda without accountability to anyone except its own membership. In comparison, religious groups that grow up affiliated, however loosely, with a parent organization run the risk of co-optation. They may, at times, find themselves representatives of the larger group to their constituent membership, advising them to wait for change rather than pressing for more immediate reform themselves. Conversely, those groups who are tied to major religious organizations stand to benefit eventually from having those organizations come around to share their position on eliminating homophobia. In that case, the affiliated groups could gain by having the moral authority and the material resources of the organizational hierarchy on their side, so to speak. It is a classic dilemma of coalition building in group politics, whether to trade access to resources and make compromises or to seek organizational independence.

DISCUSSION

The experience of the gay and lesbian rights movement within organized religion is remarkably similar to the history of the movement as a whole, and the reaction of religious communities has been consistent with their behavior in analogous situations, such as in debates over evolution. Although the movement certainly has brought about a massive net reduction in homophobia, its record is one of many successes and failures. Conversely, the religious establishment has grappled with gay and lesbian issues in much the same way it has handled other conflicts of science and beliefs.

Survey data on gays and lesbians is scant, but what information is available indicates that gay men are slightly less religious than heterosexual men. However, lesbians were considerably less religious than heterosexual females (Bell and Weinberg 1978: 149–54). Hence, the pool of potential gay and lesbian organizers within established religions may be slightly smaller than what would be found in other institutions. Nonetheless, the presence or absence of religious activity in a community appears unrelated to whether gay and lesbian organizations develop (Bainbridge 1989). Thus, the pace of organizing in religion cannot be fully explained by either a lack of personnel or religious majoritarianism.

Rather, the explanation would seem to reside in individual denominations, generally, and in separate congregations, specifically. Large-scale religious organizations roughly set the contours of what is acceptable and what is not. As would be expected, gays and lesbians have made more notable advances in participation in religious groups such as the Unitarians and the Quakers, which have a reputation for pursuing social justice, but they have made little headway in fundamentalist sects such as the evangelicals and Pentecostals.

A growing body of theological research supports the proposition that twentieth century interpretations of Biblical teachings on homosexuality are flawed. John Boswell (1980) convincingly argues that New Testament references to homosexuality condemn sexual behavior that is forced or obsessive, in much the same way heterosexuality is treated, and that Old Testament proscriptions on homosexuality have the moral force of Old Testament bans on eating shellfish. He posits the origins of Christian intolerance toward homosexuals in the twelfth century at about the time persecution of the Jews began and suggests the cause was increasing centralization in the church and demands for conformity throughout Europe. David Greenberg and Marcia Bystryn (1982), relying on an extensive literature review, concluded that the twelfth century preoccupation with homosexuality was an indirect consequence of the church's decision to enforce sacerdotal celibacy. At any rate, scholars place the dramatic rise in Christian homophobia in that time frame, and it has been in place consistently until most recently.

To the extent contemporary scholarship undermines the moral argument against homosexuality, it removes what should be the last reason for bias within religion. Scientific disapproval of gays and lesbians has already collapsed, and legal barriers are slowly falling. It is not surprising, then, that religious groups with a more humanist world view would be the first to embrace revised theological thinking, while those who insist on the preservation of more rigid dogma would look skeptically at the same body of scholarship. Thus, at the denominational level, institutions with reputations for greater social justice have been home to more advances by the gay and lesbian rights movement.

However, the importance of the individual congregation as a determining factor cannot be overlooked. Although certain denominations have reputations for liberalism or conservatism, empirical research strongly supports the proposition that individual church congregations shape the political opinions of their membership above and beyond what could be predicted from organizational affiliation alone (Wald, Owen, and Hill 1988). It implies a kind of trickle-up effect in the development of theological policy. Once gays and lesbians are included, even at the margins, of a religious organization, their presence alone should be some impetus for change. As in the women's movement, Jo Freeman (1975) found that the women positioned throughout the government were instrumental in helping to change policy. Similarly, gays and lesbians participating openly in religious affairs are well placed to influence reform. For Unitarians and Quakers the trickle up occurred quite rapidly. In most larger, more politically moderate, religious organizations, some congregations appear to be relatively accepting of gays and lesbians in their membership, and presumably what an increasing number of congregations take to be the norm would generate a demand for policy change at the top.

The rate of change will likely depend on the willingness of organized religions to evaluate traditional proscriptions on sexual behavior. Inbred homophobia makes reconsideration of traditional interpretations on Biblical references to sexuality more difficult to approach. Persons with "intrinsic" religious personalities, those who are thought to use religious values for daily decision making, have been found to be more homophobic than those with "extrinsic" personalities (Herek 1987). In a case study of a referendum vote on a gay rights ordinance in Houston, belief in the Devil was found to be a significant predictor of intolerance toward gays (Gibson and Tedin 1986). The essential point is that the overlap of religious fundamentalism and homophobia make rethinking the source of prejudice doubly difficult.

The most likely scenario would be that changes in the policies of major religious institutions will follow rather than lead changes in popular attitudes toward gays and lesbians. Large religious institutions are not likely to stray too far from majority opinion, too often for fear of losing membership to competitors in the spiritual marketplace. Spurred by declines in homophobia within individual congregations, the policies of the denominational bodies will likely accommodate gays and lesbians as they gain more acceptance in other institutional settings. Those most resistant to change will likely be the more fundamentalist sects. The path may be similar to the one observed across the twentieth century with the debate on evolution. As science undermined a traditional interpretation of the Bible, only the most ardent literalists clung to a belief in the creation myth.

Over the last century major American religious institutions have certainly changed their views on divorce and remarriage, another sexually related matter, largely in response to changing opinion in the secular environment. That is quite likely what will eventually happen with acceptance of gays and lesbians in religious institutions, but in the meantime, the discussion may sound like what was heard a few years ago in religious debate on evolution or what is said today about abortion.

Chapter 6

The Role of Religious Organizations in Evangelical Political Activity: The Moral Majority and Evangelicals for Social Action

Mel Hailey

Religious life and political life are constantly intermingling—some say meddling—in one another's affairs. On the one hand, a call goes out for strict separation of church and state. On the other, governing officials seek out religious leaders to devise plans to deal with the homeless or serve as distribution leaders for commodity food programs (i.e., cheese). Then there is the regular use of church buildings as polling stations for city, county, state, and national elections. So much for absolute separation.

The dilemma is in defining what is appropriate political behavior for those who use the language and symbols of religion in their public life and in determining how far political units can go in accommodating religion. Where are the lines drawn? What seems perfectly permissible to some is quite problematic to others. What's okay? What's not? Consensus turns into open conflict, and a call to arms is issued by both sides to resist the encroachments of the other. The battles between Jerry Falwell's

Moral Majority and Norman Lear's People For The American Way are so well known that both have become household words and caricatures of conservatives and liberals. Of course, the public policy debate is much more complex.

In recent years two organizations, both with evangelical roots, have entered debate in the public square. One group, the Moral Majority, received extensive publicity and notoriety in the popular press. The other, Evangelicals for Social Action (ESA), is not so easily recognizable by name or leadership. It is the purpose of this chapter to examine the Moral Majority[1] and Evangelicals for Social Action in the context of cultural theory. Though both groups fall into the broad category of evangelical religio-political groups, their political roles have taken vastly different paths. The styles of leadership, organization, and operation as well as issue orientation are significantly dissimilar. Specifically, I will argue that the behavior of both groups becomes more understandable in light of the cultural theory of Michael Thompson, Richard Ellis, and Aaron Wildavsky. I will not give a micro-analysis of the issue positions of either group but will instead rely on a macro approach to issues overall. This allows one to readily see the two perspectives which contrast, yet paradoxically share many similarities.

The presidential campaign of 1976 was remarkable for the manner in which candidate Jimmy Carter professed his evangelical, Southern Baptist-style of Christianity with a sincere enthusiasm. The man from Plains captured the imagination and votes of more white evangelicals than other Democratic presidential nominees in recent elections, many voting for the first time (Reichley 1985: 316, 1986: 26; Pomper 1977: 62–63; Lipset and Raab 1981: 27). Carter's frank acknowledgment of the importance of religion in his life was chronicled in his campaign autobiography *Why Not The Best?*, but his honeymoon with many of his fellow evangelical travelers was short-lived (Carter 1975). By 1980, the Moral Majority had been formed and was marshalling its resources and exhorting its constituents to aid in the defeat of the Democratic incumbent. In the *ESA Advocate*,

Ron Sider, Executive Director of ESA, wryly commented, "Well, back in 1973 we asked for evangelical political involvement—and we got the Moral Majority!" (1988: 6). The Lord works in mysterious ways.

ESA grew out of the Chicago Declaration of Social Concern in 1973. Alan Hertzke describes ESA as a "small but intellectually interesting group" whose leaders "have attempted to articulate a uniquely evangelical political witness, one which, in their view, recognizes the need to address military, social, and economic issues in terms of their own understanding of biblical principles, but which does not abandon the stress on personal morality (1988: 41). Kenneth Wald adds that ESA "was formed to capitalize on the growing willingness of theological conservatives to support social reform" (1987: 198). Thus, the Chicago Declaration reads:

God requires justice. But we have not proclaimed or demonstrated his justice to an unjust American society. Although the Lord calls us to defend the social and economic rights of the poor and oppressed, we have mostly remained silent. . . . We must attack the materialism of our culture and the maldistribution of the nation's wealth and services. We recognize that as a nation we play a crucial role in the imbalance and injustice of international trade and development. Before God and a billion hungry neighbors, we must rethink our values regarding our present standard of living and promote more just acquisition and distribution of the world's resources. . . . We must challenge the misplaced trust of the nation in economic and military might—a proud trust that promotes a national pathology of war and violence which victimizes our neighbors at home and abroad (Sider 1974: 1–2).

As Ron Sider put it, the "Evangelicals for Social Action defines its program as a consistent pro-life agenda concerned to protect the family and the environment, oppose abortion and the nuclear arms race, and seek both justice and liberty" (1987: 30). The leadership of ESA has not been very visible and is not well-known outside the evangelical community.[2] The same cannot be said for the leader of the Moral Majority.

When Jerry Falwell was reborn politically, he issued a "Declaration of War" on his television program, The Old-Time Gospel Hour. In part it read: "Be it known to all that the Old-Time Gospel Hour hereby declares war against the evils threatening America during the 1980s. Furthermore, this shall be a Holy War, not war with guns and bullets, but a war fought with the Bible, prayer and Christian involvement. The Old-Time Gospel Hour hereby dedicates itself to spearhead the battle and lead an army of Christian soldiers into the war against evil" (Chidester 1988: 279).

Falwell's rise to media stardom was meteoric. He became the feature of cover stories in national news magazines and appeared on the nightly news with great regularity. His political organization, the Moral Majority, claimed huge numbers of followers who were just awakening from their political lethargy.

Even though he is best known for his work in founding the Moral Majority, Falwell is also the head of Liberty University, pastor of the 21,000-member Thomas Road Baptist Church in Lynchburg, Virginia, and televangelist. Falwell's recipe for religion and politics became well-known: "First, get them converted; second, get them baptized; and third, get them registered to vote" (Wood 1980: 416). This is a marked about-face from the 1960s when he railed against clergy-turned-political activists.[3] Now he tells the unregistered voters in his Virginia congregation, "Repent of it. It is a sin" (Wood 1980: 416).

The Moral Majority is described (by its founder) as pro-life, pro-moral, pro-family, pro-American. It grew out of a concern that something had gone seriously wrong in America. Robert Booth Fowler described the concerns of the Moral Majority: "Abortion received approval, gay rights gained ground, and prayer or even meditation was banished from the schoolhouse. Abroad . . . atheistic communism [continued] its triumphal march and free, religious people were more and more threatened" (1985: 208). With Jerry Falwell giving a stirring defense of free enterprise, a call for military superiority over the Soviet Union, but having little to say about the care of the poor, (Falwell 1980) one can see that the Moral Majority and ESA are traveling down different lanes of the same political road.

CULTURAL THEORY

The theoretical framework for analyzing the behavior of the Moral Majority and ESA draws on the work of social anthropologist Mary Douglas. She delineates culture along two dimensions—group and grid. Group is defined by Douglas "in terms of the claims it makes over its constituent members, the boundary it draws around them, the rights it confers on them to use its name and other protections, and the levies and constraints it applies" (1982: 191). Group is the "dimension of social incorporation" (Ibid.: 190).

Grid is "the cross-hatch of rules to which individuals are subject in the course of their interaction" (Ibid.: 192), the "dimension of individuation" (Ibid.: 190). The grid is progressive. At the positive of the grid, one finds a social environment which is tightly regulated, highly prescribed, where individuals are subject to many rules regarding acceptable behavior. A low (negative) grid environment means weak prescriptions where individuals contract and bargain on their own. Classifications break down ("signs of ascribed status are scrapped one by one") (Ibid.) and "individuals are supposed to transact more and more freely" (Ibid.). The group-grid typology provides one with "a systematic comparative basis for cross-cultural studies" and serves to "enhance our understanding of social change" (Ibid.: 248).

Michael Thompson, Richard Ellis, and Aaron Wildavsky have built on the work of Douglas and applied the grid-group typology to political phenomena. In doing so, they maintain that by understanding people's cultural biases ("shared values and beliefs") (1989: 1) and the context of social relations ("patterns of interpersonal relations") (Ibid.), cultural theory allows one greater insight into preference formations. Wildavsky asserts that the way a person "answers to questions of social order—Who am I? What shall I do?" is provided by culture (1988: 6). The group holds

Figure 6-1
Models Of Four Cultures*

Prescriptions	Strength of Group Boundaries	
	Weak	*Strong*
Many	Fatalism	Hierarchy
Few	Individualism	Egalitarianism

*Adapted from Douglas and Wildavsky

the key to the "Who am I?" while the grid determines "What shall I do?"

According to Thompson, Ellis, and Wildavsky, there are five ways of life and four which correspond with the group-grid typology of Douglas. (See Figure 6-1.) Strong group boundary combined with the numerous prescriptions of the high grid result in hierarchy. Strong group but weak grid is the hallmark of egalitarianism. Individualism is found where there are few prescriptions and weak group boundaries. When group boundaries are weak and yet the people's behavior is highly prescribed, the result is fatalism. Finally, the hermit "withdraws from all the coercive social involvement in which the other four social beings, in their different ways, are caught up" (1989: 16).

Needless to say, the four ways of life offer contrasting patterns of preference. What are the cultural propensities ("preferred patterns of social relations") (Ellis and Wildavsky 1989: 6) of each of the types? Wildavsky asserts that a belief in structured inequality, social order, stability, harmony and solidarity capture the essentials of hierarchy (Ibid.). It is characterized by everyone being in his proper place. Hierarchists believe that man is born sinful but can be redeemed by good institutions: "Institutions imply permanence" (Wildavsky 1989: 106).

The egalitarian believes that man was born good but has been corrupted by evil institutions. The key theme of the egalitarian is the diminishing of differences, the promotion of equality of condition. Leaders must be rejected; after all, if one is in a position of leadership, there is an obvious inequality, i.e., leader vs. follower. When the inescapable need for a leader arises, it is for one who is charismatic. Wildavsky defines charisma as "a replacement for the law, a re-establishment of order based on the unusual personal qualities of the leader on whom the spirit of God shines or who exudes perfect egalitarian behavior" (Ibid.: 101–02). Nature is seen as ephemeral and most unforgiving by egalitarians.

Individualists are network builders who believe in a system of "bidding and bargaining" where "self-regulation reduces the need for external authority" (Wildavsky 1988: 7). Individualists accept equality of opportunity but reject any efforts moving toward equality of condition. Nature is seen as benign and "wonderfully forgiving," suggesting a laissez-faire attitude to be exerted by those in a leadership position. Leadership itself is not seen as illegitimate, à la the egalitarian model, but leadership should be restrained. The less government regulation, the less leadership, the better for the individualist. The individualist prefers a leader who knows when to leave; thus Wildavsky describes the ideal leader for an individualist as meteoric—"flame bright and burn out quickly" (Wildavsky 1989: 101).

The fatalist lives in a world that is beyond his control. He is highly prescribed but weakly bounded. Nature is capricious and unpredictable. Whatever will be, will be, for one cannot fight fate. Political preferences become irrelevant because what one wants or prefers "would not, in any event, matter" (Wildavsky 1987: 7).

A CULTURAL ANALYSIS OF THE MORAL MAJORITY AND THE ESA

I now return to the Moral Majority and ESA, but only briefly. By applying the cultural theory to the statements and actions of the Moral Majority and ESA, one should develop a more complete understanding of their political behaviors—particularly

their points of convergence and divergence. But one must first
determine an appropriate beginning point. To say that the Moral
Majority consists of free enterprise advocates and social conservatives and that ESA is solidly dedicated to the redistribution
of wealth, equality of condition, and the restructuring of evil
institutions is to do justice to neither group.

What is common to both groups? At what point could they
both meet in agreement? Both would no doubt be classified in
the religious category "evangelical Protestant" even though their
political preferences might be worlds apart. Historian Timothy
Smith calls evangelicalism a "mosaic, or suggesting even less of
an overall pattern, a kaleidoscope" (Marsden 1984: viii). George
Marsden continues, "Nonetheless, once we recognize the wide
diversity within evangelicalism and the dangers of generalization,
we may properly speak of evangelicalism as a single phenomena,"
a "transdenominational orientation" which houses the "radical
Sojourners community" as well as the "politically conservative
Moral Majority" (Ibid.). He offers several emphases which are
hallmarks of all evangelicals:

1. The Reformation doctrine of the final authority of Scripture;
2. The real historical character of God's saving work recorded in
   Scripture;
3. Eternal salvation only through personal trust in Christ;
4. The importance of evangelicalism and missions;
5. The importance of a spiritually transformed life (Ibid.).

Stephen Monsma identifies an "evangelical" as one who "believes in the historic teachings of Christianity in a literal sense and
whose beliefs shape or mold his or her actions in significant ways"
(1989: 148). He adds that "at a minimum these beliefs include
the existence of a personal, sovereign, triune God, the reality of
human sin, the authority of the Bible, and the divinity of Jesus
Christ and his death and resurrection by which the reconciliation
between God and human beings is made possible" (Ibid.).

The bedrock belief in the full authority of Scripture provides a common ground for the roots of both groups. While it is beyond the scope of this chapter to rehash two thousand years of church organizational history, it is nevertheless worthwhile to look at the central theological and cultural meeting point in history for evangelicals—the early Christian church. If the life and teachings of Jesus Christ provide the ideal, the early Christian church shows the development of Christian institutions. Evangelicals today look to Scripture as their model, and an understanding of where the early church fits in cultural theory will help in understanding where evangelicalism should fit.

Since the group boundaries of the early church are very high, two categories—fatalism and individualism—can be eliminated at the outset. Acts 2:45–48 enumerates some clearly defined means of entrance into the group.[4] The exclusion of the categories which are marked by low group identity leaves one to consider the models of hierarchy and egalitarianism. The early Christian church has often been termed an egalitarian movement, largely because of several passages which will be dealt with later, but I argue that the early Christian church corresponds more closely to hierarchy in the cultural model.

The illustration most frequently used to describe the church is that of the body, with Christ as the head and each member a part of the body with a specific function. Each part is as valuable to the body as the whole. Each has his own divinely ordained place according to his spiritual gifts (1 Cor. 12:12–31; Rom. 12:4–8). ("God has appointed first of all apostles, second prophets, third teachers, then workers of miracles, also those having gifts of healing, those able to help others, those with gifts of administration, and those speaking in different kinds of tongues") (1 Cor. 12: 28–30).

Along with distinctions of gifts and ministry, there is a prescribed hierarchy of authority: hierarchy of leadership within the church, hierarchy within the family, and hierarchy within social relationships. In Timothy 2 and 3, Paul spells out to Timothy the lines of authority in the church: God, Christ Jesus, the apostles,

overseers (bishops or elders), and deacons, and men in general.
Members are told to follow the teachings and traditions handed
down from the apostles (2 Thess. 2:15) and to honor those who
serve as bishops or overseers (1 Tim. 5:17).

Neither are women left without prescriptive roles. Women are
not to be in authority over men, overseers' wives are to conduct
themselves in accordance with certain standards of behavior,
wives are to submit to the authority of their husbands, and there
are even roles for the older and younger women (Titus 2:3–4).
Those on the bottom level of the hierarchy are given instruction
to obey and submit to those in authority over them as they would
submit to Jesus. Children are told to obey and honor their parents
(Eph. 6:1), and slaves are told to obey their masters. In keeping
with the importance of this hierarchy of leadership, loose as it
may seem, it is interesting to note that the first official act of
the tiny band of Christians was the selection of Matthias as a
replacement for the position given up by the desertion and death
of Judas Iscariot (Acts 1).

Peter and Paul both understood their power to be strictly
limited, in subordination to Jesus, and saw themselves in a
secondary position. Authority was not placed in the person but
in the position. Paul has to make appeal in numerous passages to
the authenticity of his apostleship (Gal. 1 and 2; 2 Cor. 11–5; Eph.
3:7–11), evidently because it is questioned regularly. Paul needs
others such as Barnabas to corroborate his credentials (Acts 9:27;
10:25). Peter refers to himself as "a fellow elder" under the "Chief
Shepherd" (1 Pet. 5:104), seeing his personal power as limited,
as did Paul, who found it necessary to rebuke Peter publicly in
Jerusalem for drawing back from the Gentiles he had previously
welcomed into the church (Gal. 3:28).

The egalitarian view of man, which sees man as basically
good but corrupted by evil institutions, is perhaps the most
clear-cut exception to the placing of the early church in the
egalitarian mode (Thompson, Ellis and Wildavsky 1989: 20).
This is strongly contradicted by early church doctrine (Rom. 3:10,
22–23). However, there are passages in the New Testament

which appear to lend a strong egalitarian flavor to the early church. These can be divided into two categories: the "holding all things common" (economic equality), and the teaching that in Jesus there is "neither bond nor free, Jew nor Greek, male nor female" (social equality). Both categories must be examined in the context of the first century setting.

The true egalitarian society is concerned with the diminishing of distinctions between peoples, with the goal of making conditions equal for all. The first few chapters of Acts, which detail the beginning of the Christian church, stress that the sharing of all things and the selling of lands in order to give the money to the apostles was not for the purpose of redistributing all the wealth equally, but rather for the purpose of making sure that there were no needy among the members of the church. The idea of a safety net comes to mind as more appropriately describing the intent of the early Christians. Redistributive programs were not aimed at leveling society, but at taking care of those with a specific need.

Second, those who see the early Christian church as an egalitarian organization often point to Paul's statement, "There is neither Jew nor Greek, slave nor free, male nor female, for you are all one in Christ Jesus" (Gal. 3:28). While this statement smacks at the heart of egalitarian thinking on the surface, there is an alternative explanation which makes sense in terms of hierarchy. Paul is talking about the equality of worth in the eyes of God, but he in no way tries to eliminate the distinctions evident in the prevailing way of life or to institute a new social ordering. Thus Paul, in good conscience, can tell the slave Onesimus to return to his master Philemon,[5] can place numerous prescriptions on women regarding their position within the church (1 Cor. 11:3, 14:33–35), and urge his correspondents to be submissive to those in positions of authority whether it be the government (Rom. 13:1–7; Titus 3:1–2), the private sector, or in the home (Col. 3:18–21).

In short, Paul seems to be telling church members that their behavior should reflect respect toward the major institutions of the day and that every person should work within his proper place in society. Peter reinforces the work of Paul when he writes, "Submit yourselves for the Lord's sake to every authority instituted among men: whether to the king, as the supreme authority, or to governors" (1 Pet. 2:13–14). This is certainly not good news for a radical egalitarian.

Now back to the Moral Majority and ESA. I argue that the behavior of both groups is understandable if one accepts that both are historically rooted in hierarchy. There is no attempt to flesh out any particular degree of hierarchy. Second, the more conservative Moral Majority retains a commitment to hierarchy but accepts some features of individualism. Third, ESA also retains a weakened commitment to hierarchy but shows a pronounced shift to egalitarianism.

THE MORAL MAJORITY AND ESA
AS HIERARCHY

There are two substantial points of agreement between the Moral Majority and ESA I wish to make on the matter of hierarchy. First, neither the Moral Majority nor ESA would deny the sinful nature of man. Ed Dobson, a professor at Liberty University and one-time leader in the Moral Majority writes, "Fundamentalists believe in the depravity of human nature" (1987: 14). There is no disagreement among fundamentalists on the question. This is only slightly different from the tack taken in a statement developed by the ESA Board of Directors which reads in part, "Realizing that because of the Fall human beings are in bondage to sin, we repudiate secular plans to transform society through mere structural change and environmental improvement" (Sider 1987: 205). Both are squarely within the tradition of the early Christian church.

Second, when Jerry Falwell emphasizes that there are three institutions ordained by God—the government, the family, and the church—ESA is in agreement. And when ESA argues "that the restraining hand of government can reduce the ways sin becomes embedded in socio-economic systems" (Ibid.: 206), the Moral Majority concurs. Of course, each promotes a different governmental approach to problems. In any event, the acceptance of the legitimacy of societal institutions, coupled with the rights of those institutions to prescribe certain standards of behavior within their sphere of influence, is characteristic of high grid groups.

The social conservatism of both groups makes sense if explained by a commitment to hierarchy. The Moral Majority and ESA can view abortion as a rejection of the authority of God, the Creator of life. The ESA beliefs and commitment statement reads, "Recognizing creation as the gift of the triune God, who makes persons in His own image, we accept His mandate to be faithful stewards of the earth and to respect the sacredness of human life" (Ibid.: 205). God made the rule, it was within his sphere to do so, and it is the proper place of man to obey. No argument here for the Moral Majority or ESA, even over the language used by a couple of the leaders to oppose abortion. Ron Sider stated, "Abortion and infanticide are murder. In a pluralistic society people should be free to do many things that others consider stupid or sinful. But tolerance toward others does not extend to allowing them to kill other people" (Ibid.: 55–6). Jerry Falwell joins in chorus: "Abortion is not birth control nor family planning. It is murder according to the Word of God" (Falwell 1980: 14). Abortion is seen as a form of deviant behavior which must be stopped unless there are exceptional circumstances where the life of the mother is threatened.

Forms of behavior that threaten the family are strongly objectionable to both the Moral Majority and ESA, such as the evils of pornography, homosexual behavior, and secular humanism. A review of positions from the Moral Majority and ESA shows no major points of disagreement here. ESA maintains, "The family is the pre-eminent social institution for inculcating the values and beliefs on which an unchaining democracy depends. This includes obedience to legitimate authority and a sense of duty and responsibility toward others" (Sider 1987: 126). Falwell relates the strength of the nation to the strength of families in the nation.

THE MORAL MAJORITY GOES TO MARKET

First and foremost the Moral Majority is a product of its fundamentalist evangelical heritage. The Moral Majority may have burst upon the political scene like Joshua's trumpet-blasting army, but it is not a new phenomenon. What is an interesting twist is how the Moral Majority has tried to reach beyond the fundamentalist borders of its organizers. This is no easy trick, given the separatist nature of fundamentalist theology.

The nation's history is replete with religio-political experiences that might well be considered predecessors of the current movement. Martin F. Marty suggests that if the major emphasis of the Moral Majority is to restore a Christian America, one can point to July 4, 1827, when Philadelphia Presbyterian Ezra Stiles Ely proclaimed that "every ruler should be an avowed and sincere friend of Christianity" and advocated "a Christian party in politics" (1982: 98). Another antecedent to the Moral Majority is the prohibition movement organization, the Anti-Saloon League, which was little more than a front for the Methodist Church. Other ancestors include late nineteenth-century evangelists who called for the return of Palestine to the Jews and seventeenth-century religionists who established the concept of America as a chosen nation of God (Ibid.: 98–99).

Though there are many possible precedents, it appears that the New Religious Right (NRR) is the cultural descendant of early twentieth-century fundamentalists who led the fight against modernity (Hofstadter 1963: 117–41). Protestantism split into two opposing camps with the rise of the social gospel. Walter Rauschenbusch, a leading proponent of this movement, explained the term as follows:

Sin is essentially selfishness. That definition is more in harmony with the social gospel than with any individualistic type of religion. The sinful mind, then, is the unsocial and anti-social mind. To find the climax of sin we must not linger over a man who swears, or sneers, at religion, or denies the mystery of the trinity, but put our hands on social groups who have turned the patrimony of the nation into the private property of a small class, or have left the peasant labourers cowed, degraded, demoralized, and without rights in the land. When we find such in history, or in present-day life, we shall know we have struck real rebellion against God on the higher levels of sin (Webber 1981: 60).

Fundamentalists rejected this notion and saw themselves as the defenders of orthodox theology. However, by the time of the 1925 Scopes trial and the great confrontation between Clarence Darrow and William Jennings Bryan, fundamentalists were often seen as unenlightened, anti-intellectual, intolerant bigots (Neuhaus 1982: 19). Out of the spotlight, fundamentalism flourished. The doctrine was by no means diluted, but political activity was eschewed. Christian responsibility to government could be summarized by three words: pay, pray and obey. To be sure, followers were encouraged to oppose Al Smith's candidacy in 1928 and support Prohibition. For the most part, however, there was no systematic political philosophy. George Marsden contends that they "responded to the issues haphazardly and on the basis of inherited prejudice and formulae, with next to no theoretical preparation to guide them" (1980: 209). The drift toward political conservatism came out of a culture based on reaction to liberal theology, which was seen as an ally of liberal politicians.

The fundamentalist doctrine that keeps Jerry Falwell tightly bounded as the pastor of the Thomas Road Baptist Church presented an obstacle for him in the exercising of leadership in a broader political context where there is no purity of the group. Marsden recognized the dilemma facing fundamentalists as that of "separation from unbelief" (Douglas and Tipton 1983: 153). Can ministers of different faiths cooperate politically, even if they can't agree on theology? If the answer is no, then one is left with a very narrow base and limited effectiveness. If the answer is yes, then networking can take place. One can move to the marketplace and try to sell a political ideology to all who wish to purchase. Jerry Falwell and the Moral Majority developed an ingenious way to bridge the boundary that would allow him to remain theologically pure in the competition of the marketplace.

The Moral Majority was not a religious organization! Ed Dobson emphasizes this point when he writes, "The unique dimension of Moral Majority is that it is *not* a religious organization" (1987: 3). Jerry Falwell made the same point at a Washington press conference: "We're not a theological organization" (Willoughby 1981: 44). By separating the political form from the religious, the Moral Majority could join with non-fundamentalists to pursue a common political agenda. The leaders of the Moral Majority, by maintaining that the organization was not religious, were able to bring together religion and politics. Richard Viguerie writes that Falwell's purpose was

to build a coalition of not only his own religious followers but of Catholics, Jews and Mormons. Significantly, New Right leaders Paul Weyrich, an Eastern Rite Catholic, and Howard Phillips, a Jew, worked closely with Falwell in setting up the Moral Majority. The potential of such a coalition is tremendous. There are an estimated 85 million Americans—50 million born again Protestants, 30 million morally conservative Catholics, 3 million Mormons and 2 million Orthodox and Conservative Jews—with whom to build a pro-family, Bible-believing coalition (1981: 129).

Falwell justified his action to the press by stating, "We're a moral organization. No one has to violate his integrity by becoming involved" (Willoughby 1981: 44). Jerry Falwell bridged the gulf that separated fundamentalists from other non-fundamentalists or even non-evangelical religions.

In the political arena, Falwell could network with other New Right groups. This became very evident at the National Affairs Briefing. Scheduled for Dallas in August 1980, the National Affairs Briefing received heavy national media coverage. All three presidential candidates, Jimmy Carter, John Anderson, and Ronald Reagan, were invited to address the 15,000 persons who attended, but only candidate Reagan accepted. The Dallas event turned out to be much more than just a speech by one presidential candidate. Virtually all organizations in the family of NRR were represented, distributing literature and exhorting the faithful. Besides Reagan, keynote addresses were given by Representative Phil Crane, Senator Jesse Helms, Phyllis Schlafly of the Eagle Forum, Paul Weyrich from the Committee for the Survival of a Free Congress, James Robison of the Roundtable, Pat Robertson of the 700 Club, and of course, Jerry Falwell representing the Moral Majority.

Other characteristics of individualism are also apparent in the Moral Majority, particularly an unswerving acceptance of the free enterprise system. Falwell argues that the work ethic, competition in business, ambition and successful business management are all given biblical sanction in Proverbs. However, Falwell never really develops his scriptural position, never actually citing specific references in Proverbs. Instead, the leader of the Moral Majority shifts to secular authors to support his case, liberally quoting the economic views of Milton Friedman and William Simon (Falwell 1980: 12).

When the entrepreneurial spirit hit Falwell, he rose rapidly to stardom. Some say that he was simply in the right place at the right time. I take exception to that explanation because this is so characteristic of leadership in an individualistic culture. Jerry Falwell and the Moral Majority reacted strongly to the threat of secularization. He moved in, played by the established rules of an interest group society, and got out. Like George Washington Plunkitt, Falwell "seen his opportunities and took 'em."

As a competitor in the market, he was motivated and fierce. In 1984 he surprised some by endorsing George Bush, a mainline Episcopalian, over another evangelical leader active in NRR politics, Rev. Pat Robertson. To survive, though, one had best go with the favorite and be careful about long shots.

One must also know when to leave. On June 11, 1989, Jerry Falwell announced that the Moral Majority was formally disbanding. He said that the mission was accomplished and the "organization is no longer needed" (Briggs 1989: 3B). Terminating the Moral Majority was another step in Falwell's withdrawal from politics to devote more time to his work at Liberty University and Thomas Road Baptist Church. At the outset of his foray into the political arena, he defended his politicization as a temporary move to ensure that Christianity would be able to survive in the United States (Fowler 1985: 97). Like a good individualist leader, when the crisis or opportunities for growth were past, he stepped back.

ESA: PURITY MAINTAINED

ESA represents an interesting contrast to the individualism of the Moral Majority. Whereas the Moral Majority lessened the ties that bind, ESA has maintained its high group posture. When ESA bears witness, it does so as a vehicle for religious fellow travelers. Fowler wryly comments that ESA is one of those evangelical organizations that serve as a "source of sharp criticism of the Christian Right" (1985: 226). Since the Moral Majority is no longer within the confines of the group, severe criticism is not only understandable but expected. There is not even the pretense made that ESA is not a religious organization. Every action, every issue position, every pronouncement is justified by Scripture, or what Sider terms a "balanced Biblical agenda" which is completely pro-life (Sider 1987: 28).

When Jerry Falwell was quoted in a *Christianity Today* interview, "We could never bring up the issue of the poor in Moral Majority. . . . We just have to stay away from helping the poor," the executive director of ESA was incredulous at such a statement (Ibid.). Sider was quick to point out, "That simply will not do if Jerry Falwell wants a biblical pro-life agenda. According to God's Word, human life matters after birth as well as before" (Ibid.). In a low group arena, Falwell's actions are quite justifiable—one has freedom to bargain, to select, to reject positions at will. There is no such corresponding luxury in a high group context. Getting away from essentials that bond the group are totally unacceptable. Thus a greater burden is on ESA to remain pure than on the Moral Majority.

But even in ESA there is cultural movement, not from hierarchy to individualism, but from hierarchy to egalitarianism. Can ESA make this transition and remain true to its early Christian church model? I suggest that group, not grid, is the key. ESA does not reject hierarchy as it moves toward egalitarianism. Instead, it seeks egalitarian results through hierarchical processes while maintaining a critical posture toward both. ESA is best characterized as a weak hierarchical and weak egalitarian organization. The boundaries of ESA are determined by its interpretation of Scripture, which adapts the early Christian church to a mixture of hierarchy and egalitarianism. It also leads to several "on the one hand—on the other hand" views. To explain this more fully I look at the ESA view of authority and institutions, and pronouncements on equality.

As mentioned earlier, ESA has no problem accepting that there are certain institutions ordained by God, including the government and the family. Vernon Grounds explains the importance of government to ESA members in the *ESA Advocate*, the organization's monthly publication: "Without government, God's redemptive purpose could not be achieved; without government, human beings, fallen and selfish, would subsist in a state of animal-like conflict" (1988: 8). He continues, "Christians therefore recognize that even a very imperfect, corrupt, and bungling government reflects divine majesty. It mirrors the saving will of the all-righteous God—though often like a mud puddle mirrors the shining splendor of the sun!" (Ibid.). Criticism and acceptance are both allowed:

Granted that inefficiency, incompetence, and injustice sometimes exist—from the city council on up to the higher echelons of our federal establishment in Washington, D.C.—and that deplorable corruption is sometimes exposed, Christians must still refuse to countenance cynicism and contempt with respect to government. Although there will be times when Christians may need to protest a government's actions and disobey laws that violate God's standards, Christians must nevertheless affirm that behind all the pettiness and graft of power-hungry people stands the immutable majesty of the One who is the source and sanction of all righteousness, order, and justice. In short, respect for law ought to characterize Christians; it ought to be an attitude they strive to exhibit by word and example (Ibid.: 10–11).

Sider echoes Grounds in that "it is government, not the individual, who bears the sword (Romans 13:4). If we allow individuals to take the law into their own hands, society degenerates into anarchy" (1989: 2).

But what about a system where evil flourishes? The general pattern found in ESA material is that decentralization of power provides the better way. If it can be accomplished, there should be less reliance on rigid structures where procedures are stressed more than fundamental principles of justice and fairness. A case in point is the crisis in the American criminal justice system. The ESA criticism follows: "American criminal justice, unlike biblical justice, is built on the notion that peace is equivalent to public order. It views crime as an offense against government, not an injury to the victim or community. It does not require that victims be repaid, that offenders make things right, or that the community take responsibility to see justice done" (Van Ness 1988: 3A).

The solution in part: "First, bring victims back into center stage in the criminal justice process" (Ibid.). How is this accomplished? The solution is an anti-authoritarian, "Couldn't they be allowed to file as plaintiffs along with the government in criminal cases? . . . Victims better represent their own interests in a criminal trial than government currently does" (Ibid.).

The family is central to ESA. It is seen as "essential for abundant living," and a "divine gift." Right relationships are stressed; there is a proper ordering and lines of authority within each family unit. The problems with the family are not that the institution is flawed but that society no longer practices correct forms of behavior. "Western society is sick. Through decades of obstinate rebellion against God's intention, modern folk have lost the joy of sexuality and the security, happiness and fulfillment of the family. Divorce, spouse and child abuse, and sexual perversion run rampant. Agony and hell haunt our homes."[6]

The shoring up of the family is more of a function of hierarchy where everyone is in their proper place. The correctly structured family is not one in which the husband is an autocrat, but where there is "mutual interdependence between man and woman" (Sider 1987: 108).

Egalitarians are concerned with diminishing inequalities. Wildavsky writes, "The best indicator of egalitarian practices, therefore, is their attempt to reduce differences—between races, or income levels, or sexes etc." (1988: 9). ESA pursues just such an agenda, including sexual equality. All ESA writings share a common theme that God shows a special concern for the poor, the downtrodden, the widow, the orphan, the dispossessed; so should Christians. If individual action can help achieve such results, then individual action is called for. If there are structural evils that perpetuate inequality, the structures should be changed. It should be noted that structural evil is not limited to governmental or economic systems, but can also be found in the church. Thus the Chicago Declaration takes the evangelicals to task over civil rights: "We deplore the historic involvement of the church in America with racism and the conspicuous responsibility of the evangelical community for perpetuating the personal attitudes and institutional structures that have divided the body of Christ along color lines. Further, we have failed to condemn the exploitation of racism at home and abroad by our economic system" (Sider 1974: 1–2).

In the past year there have been 17 articles or newsnotes in the *ESA Advocate* on the evils of racism. ESA has been particularly outspoken over apartheid, and has called for sanctions against South Africa, a boycott of Shell, and participation in public rallies and vigils to bring attention to the injustices of apartheid.

Perhaps the best statement of ESA's working within the egalitarian framework already described is found in the statement that is an affirmation of the principles of ESA as adopted by the board of directors:

We oppose governments of the left and right which violate human rights, ignore religious and political freedoms, or neglect the needs of the poor. We oppose abortion on demand which destroys millions of lives each year. We oppose, as well, the escalating arms race which increasingly threatens to annihilate millions of human beings made in God's image. We support all strategies and agencies that strengthen the family and support the view that marriage is a life-long covenant between one man and one woman. We seek to be informed about and responsive to human suffering that results from oppressive and unjust economic systems. We seek an end to institutionalized racism and discrimination based on ethnicity, gender, age or physical ability. We seek to preserve and extend democratic systems and the freedoms upon which democracies are based (Ibid.: 207).

Even here, however, the fact that there are still elements of hierarchy is indicative of the dilemma facing ESA within the American political system. There is no doubt that the Moral Majority found a home in the Republican party even if highly favored Republican officeholders did not deliver on many of the issues of importance. ESA postures itself in a rather uncomfortable position suspended between hierarchy and egalitarianism. At the national level the platforms of both the Democratic and Republican parties pose great concern, one that has no easy resolution. Since cultural theory tells us that ways of life are in competition, ESA is in a very unenviable situation if hierarchists view ESA with suspicion because of its egalitarian tendencies, and egalitarians are bothered by the association with hierarchy. Faced with a strong and consistent pro-life political agenda, alas, ESA is culturally torn. On the other hand, the Moral Majority burned hot in the individualist camp. It could use others and be used by others as it bid and bargained on a wide and perhaps less consistent range of political issues. Eventually, it burned out.

Notes

CHAPTER 4

1. Professor James L. Guth of Furman University informs me that more recent scholarship has called into question whether the earliest Christians were all pacifists. But the argument of this chapter does not hinge on that question, one way or the other.

2. This research has been conducted as part of a project funded by the United States Institute of Peace. The larger project is being conducted in collaboration with Professor Byron Johnson of Memphis State University. The opinions, findings, and conclusions or recommendations expressed in this chapter are those of the author and do not necessarily reflect the views of the United States Institute of Peace or those of Professor Johnson.

CHAPTER 6

1. Before the Moral Majority formally disbanded in June 1989, it had assumed the name Liberty Foundation. This chapter will refer to the

organization by its better-known name.

2. The President of ESA is Vernon Grounds; Executive Director, Ron Sider; Chairperson of the Board of Directors, Tony Campolo. Members of the National Advisory Board include Senator Mark Hatfield; John Perkins, of the Voice of Calvary Ministries; and Jim Wallis, Editor of *Sojourners*.

3. A sermon preached on Sunday, March 21, 1965, is the best example of Falwell's criticism of preachers becoming political activists. In it he denounced the activities of civil rights leaders, specifically mentioning by name Dr. Martin Luther King, Jr., and Mr. James Farmer. An excerpt reflects Falwell's position: "Our only purpose on this earth is to know Christ and to make him known. Believing the Bible as I do, I would find it impossible to stop preaching the pure saving grace of Jesus Christ, and begin doing anything else—including fighting communism, or participating in civil rights reforms. . . . Preachers are not called upon to be politicians but to be soul winners." See Perry Deane Young, *God's Bullies* (New York: Holt, Rinehart and Winston, 1982), 310–317, for the full text of Falwell's sermon.

4. All Scripture references are taken from the New International Version.

5. See Philemon. Also in 1 Timothy 6:1 Paul writes, "All who are under the yoke of slavery should consider their masters worthy of full respect . . . " and in Ephesians 6:5, "Slaves, obey your earthly masters with respect and fear, and with sincerity of heart just as you would obey Christ." Titus 2:9 reads, "Teach slaves to be subject to their masters in everything . . . " and in Colossians 3:22 the message is repeated, "Slaves, obey your earthly masters in everything."

6. Radical feminists are described by Sider as "extreme feminists who describe heterosexuality as rape, motherhood as slavery, and all relations between men and women as a power struggle. The traditional family is the enemy. The solution is lesbianism, industrialization of housework, and public care of children from birth" (Sider 1987: 119).

Bibliography

Abrams, Ray H. 1969. *Preachers Present Arms: The Role of the American Churches and Clergy in World Wars I and II, with Some Observations on the War in Vietnam.* Scottsdale, Pennsylvania: Herald Press.

Adam, B. D. 1987. *The Rise of a Gay and Lesbian Movement.* Boston: Twanye Publishers.

Bainbridge, W. S. 1989. "The Religious Ecology of Deviance." *American Sociological Review* 54: 288–95.

Bainton, Roland H. 1960. *Christian Attitudes Toward War and Peace: A Historical Survey and Critical Re-Evaluation.* Nashville: Abingdon Press.

Basta. December 1985. National Newsletter of the Chicago Religious Task Force On Central America.

Basta. June 1986. National Newsletter of the Chicago Religious Task Force On Central America.

Basta. September 1986. National Newsletter of the Chicago Religious Task Force On Central America.

Basta. December 1986. National Newsletter of the Chicago Religious Task Force On Central America.

Basta. June 1987. National Newsletter of the Chicago Religious Task Force On Central America.

Basta. December 1987. National Newsletter of the Chicago Religious Task Force On Central America.

Bauer, Raymond A., de Sola Pool, Ithiel, and Dexter, Lewis A. 1968. *American Business and Public Policy*. New York: Atherton Press.

Bell, A. P. and Weinberg, M. S. 1978. *Homosexualities: A Study of Diversity Among Men and Women*. New York: Simon and Schuster.

Berry, Jeffrey M. 1977. *Lobbying for the People*. Princeton: Princeton University Press.

Bibby, John F., Mann, Thomas E., and Ornstein, Norman J. eds. 1980. *Vital Statistics on Congress, 1980*. Washington, D.C.: American Enterprise Institute.

Blair, R. 1982. *Evangelicals (?!) Concerned*. New York: Ralph Blair.

Boswell, J. 1980. *Christianity, Social Tolerance, and Homosexuality*. Chicago: University of Chicago Press.

Briggs, David. June 12, 1989. *The Contra-Costa Times*. 3B.

Carter, Jimmy. 1975. *Why Not The Best?* New York: Bantam Books.

Cater, Douglass. 1964. *Power in Washington*. New York: Random House.

Catholic Agitator. August 1984.

Central America Resource Center. 1984. *Directory of Central America Organizations*. Austin.

Central America Resource Center. 1985. *Directory of Central America Organizations*. Austin.

Central America Resource Center. 1987. *Directory of Central America Organizations*. Austin.

Chatfield, Charles. 1971. *For Peace and Justice: Pacifism in America, 1914–1941*. Knoxville: University of Tennessee Press.

Chidester, David. 1988. *Patterns of Power: Religion and Politics in American Culture*. Englewood Cliffs, New Jersey: Prentice-Hall.

Churchill, Winston S. 1948. *The Gathering Storm*. Volume I of VI in *The Second World War*. Boston: Houghton Mifflin Co.

Cohen, David and Wolff, Wendy. 1980. "Freeing Congress from the

Special Interest State: A Public Interest Agenda for the 1980s." *Harvard Journal on Legislation* 17: 253–293.

Costain, Anne N. December 1980. "The Struggle for a National Women's Lobby: Organizing a Diffuse Interest." *Western Political Quarterly* 33: 476–491.

CRTFCA. 1988. *Information Pamphlet.* Chicago: Chicago Religious Task Force On Central America.

Dahl, Robert A. 1961. *Who Governs?* New Haven: Yale University Press.

Damas, R. Y. December 1986. "To Return the Persecuted to the Source, the Origin, the Cause of Their Suffering is an Act of Injustice in the Eyes of Christian Love." *Basta*: 24–25.

DeBenedetti, Charles. 1980. *The Peace Reform in American History.* Bloomington: Indiana University Press.

D'Emilio, J. 1983. *Sexual Politics, Sexual Communities.* Chicago: University of Chicago Press.

Dobson, Ed. 1987. "The Bible, Politics, and Democracy." In *The Bible, Politics, and Democracy*, ed. Richard John Neuhaus. Grand Rapids, Michigan: William B. Eerdmanns Publishing Company.

Douglas, Mary. 1982. *In The Active Voice.* London: Routledge & Kegan Paul.

Douglas, Mary and Tipton, Steven, eds. 1983. *Religion and America.* Boston: Beacon Press.

Edwards, C. 1981. *Hugo Grotius, the Miracle of Holland.* Chicago: Nelson-Hall.

Edwards, C. L. 1983. "Political Asylum and Withholding of Deportation: Defining the Appropriate Standard of Proof Under the Refugee Act of 1980." *San Diego Law Review* 21: 171–184.

Ellis, Richard and Wildavsky, Aaron. 1989. *Dilemmas of Presidential Leadership from Washington Through Lincoln.* New Brunswick, New Jersey: Transaction Publishers.

Falwell, Jerry. 1980. *Listen America!* New York: Bantam Books.

Fowler, Robert B. 1985. *Religion and Politics in America.* Metuchen, New Jersey: The Scarecrow Press, Inc.

Freeman, J. 1975. *The Politics of Women's Liberation.* New York: David McKay Co.

Freiberg, P. March 15, 1988. "Gay Catholics Arrested as Protests Continue at St. Patrick's." *The Advocate*: 18.

Freiberg, P. March 29, 1988. "Episcopal Diocese in New Jersey

Approves Blessing of Gay Relationships." *The Advocate*: 13.

Freiberg, P. August 16, 1988. "New Outreach or Publicity Ploy?" *The Advocate*: 13.

Frohlich, Norman, Oppenheimer, Joe, and Young, Oran. 1971. *Political Leadership and Collective Goods*. Princeton: Princeton University Press.

Gardner, John W. 1972. *In Common Cause*. New York: W. W. Norton & Co.

Gayellow Pages. 1990. New York: Renaissance House.

Gibson, J. L. and Tedin, K. T. 1986. "Political Tolerance and the Rights of Homosexuals: A Contextual Analysis." Paper presented at the Annual Meeting of the Midwest Political Science Association, Chicago.

Golden, R. and McConnell, M. 1986. *Sanctuary: The New Underground Railroad*. New York: Orbis Books.

Greenberg, D. F. and Bystryn, M. H. 1982. "Christian Intolerance of Homosexuality." *American Journal of Sociology* 88: 515–48.

Grimes, B. and Kaiser, G. n.d. *Gay Rights Movement in The Religious Society of Friends*. Sumneytown, Pennsylvania: Friends for Lesbian and Gay Concerns.

Grounds, Vernon. November/December 1988. "Amphibious Christians." *ESA Advocate*: 8.

Harding, R. June 21, 1988. "Methodists Reject Three Proposals to Relax Church's Antigay Stance." *The Advocate*: 10–12.

Harding, R. June 19, 1990. "Methodists Clash Over Gay Marriage." *The Advocate*: 14.

Hays, Samuel P. October 1964. "The Politics of Reform in Municipal Government in the Progressive Era." *Pacific Northwest Quarterly* 55: 157–169.

Helton, A. C. 1984. "Political Asylum Under the 1980 Refugee Act: An Unfulfilled Promise." *University of Michigan Law Reference* 17: 243–264.

Helton, A. C. 1985. "The Proper Role of Discretion in Political Asylum Determinations." *San Diego Law Review* 22: 999–1020.

Herek, G. M. 1987. "Religious Orientation and Prejudice: A Comparison of Racial and Sexual Attitudes." *Personality and Social Psychology Bulletin* 13: 34–44.

Hertzke, Allen D. 1988. *Representing God In Washington*. Knoxville: University of Tennessee Press.

Hofstadter, Richard. 1955. *The Age of Reform: From Bryan to F.D.R.* New York: Vintage.

Hofstadter, Richard. 1963. *Anti-Intellectualism in American Life.* New York: Alfred A. Knopf.

Katz, J. 1976. *Gay American History.* New York: Avon Books.

Leonard, A. S. 1989. *Gay and Lesbian Civil Rights Protections In The U.S.* Washington, D.C.: National Gay and Lesbian Task Force.

Lindblom, Charles E. 1977. *Politics and Markets.* New York: Basic Books.

Lindblom, Charles S. 1980. *The Policy-Making Process.* 2nd ed. Englewood Cliffs, New Jersey: Prentice-Hall.

Lipset, Seymour M. and Raab, Earl. March 1981. "The Election & the Evangelicals." *Commentary* 71: 27.

Lipsky, Michael. 1968. "Protest as a Political Resource." *American Political Science Review* 62: 144–58.

Loder, T. 1986. *No One But Us.* San Diego: Luramedia.

Loescher, G., and Scanlan, J. A. 1986. *Calculated Kindness.* New York: Free Press.

Lowi, Theodore J. July 1964. "American Business, Public Policy, Case Studies, and Political Theory." *World Politics* 16: 677–715.

Lowi, Theodore J. 1971. *The Politics of Disorder.* New York: Basic Books.

Lowi, Theodore J. 1979. *The End of Liberalism.* 2nd Ed. New York: W. W. Norton & Co.

Manchester, William. 1988. *The Last Lion: Winston Spencer Churchill; Alone: 1932–1940.* Boston: Little, Brown and Co.

Marsden, George M. 1980. *Fundamentalism and American Culture: The Shaping of the Twentieth Century Evangelism 1870–1925.* New York: Oxford University Press.

Marsden, George M. 1984. *Evangelism and Modern America.* Grand Rapids, Michigan: William B. Eerdmans Publishing Company.

Marty, Martin E. February/March 1982. "Precursors of the Moral Majority." *American Heritage* 33: 2 98–99.

Marx, Gary T. 1969. *Protest and Prejudice.* New York: Harper & Row Torchbooks.

Mayhew, David R. 1974. *Congress: The Electoral Connection.* New Haven: Yale University Press.

McCarry, Charles. 1972. *Citizen Nader.* New York: Saturday Review Press.

McConnell, Grant. 1953. *The Decline of Agrarian Democracy*. Berkeley: University of California Press.

McConnell, Grant. 1966. *Private Power and American Democracy*. New York: Alfred A. Knopf.

McConnell, Michael. June 1986. "Bringing the War Home." *Basta*: 7–14.

McFarland, Andrew S. 1976. *Public Interest Lobbies: Decision Making on Energy*. Washington, D.C.: American Enterprise Institute.

McFarland, Andrew S. 1978. " 'Third Forces' in American Politics: The Case of Common Cause." In *Parties and Elections in an Anti-Party Age*, ed. Jeff Fishel. Bloomington: University of Indiana Press.

McFarland, Andrew S. 1980. *Public Interest Lobbies*. Washington, D.C.: American Enterprise Institute for Public Policy Research.

McFarland, Andrew S. 1983. *Common Cause*. Chatham, New Jersey: Chatham House.

McFarland, Andrew S. 1983. "Public Interest Lobbies Versus Minority Faction." In *Interest Group Politics*, eds. A. J. Cigler and B. A. Loomis, pp. 324–353. Washington: Congressional Quarterly Press.

McFarland, Andrew S. 1987. "Interest Groups and Theories of Power in America." *British Journal of Political Science* 17: 129–147.

Meyer, Donald B. 1960. *The Protestant Search for Political Realism, 1919–1941*. Berkeley: University of California Press.

Miliband, Ralph. 1969. *The State in Capitalist Society*. New York: Basic Books.

Miller, Robert M. 1971. *How Shall They Hear Without a Preacher?: The Life of Ernest Fremont Tittle*. Chapel Hill: University of North Carolina Press.

Mitchell, Robert C. April 1980. "How 'Soft,' 'Deep,' or 'Left?' Present Constituencies in the Environmental Movement for Certain World Views." *Natural Resources Journal* 20: 346.

Moe, Terry M. 1980. *The Organization of Interests*. Chicago: University of Chicago Press.

Monsma, Stephen. 1989. "The Promise and Pitfalls of Evangelical Political Involvement." In *Contemporary Evangelical Political Involvement*, ed. Corwin E. Smidt. New York: University Press of America.

Nadel, Mark V. 1971. *The Politics of Consumer Protection*. Indianapolis: Bobbs-Merrill Co.

National Gay Pentecostal Alliance. 1990. *What is the National Gay Pentecostal Alliance?* Schenectady, New York: National Gay Pentecostal Alliance.

National Lawyers Guild. June 6, 1986. *Central American Refugee Defense Fund Newsletter*.

Neuhaus, Richard J. March 19, 1982. "Who, Now, Will Shape the Meaning of America?" *Christianity Today*: 19.

Niebuhr, Reinhold. 1940. *Christianity and Power Politics*. New York: Charles Scribner's Sons.

North American FLGC. 1988. *Friends for Lesbian and Gay Concerns*. Sumneytown, Pennsylvania: FLGC.

Nuttall, Geoffrey. 1958. *Christian Pacifism in History*. London: Basil Blackwell & Mott, Ltd.

Office of Lesbian and Gay Concerns, UUA. 1990. *Welcoming Congregation Program*. Boston: OLGC.

Olson, Mancur, Jr. 1965. *The Logic of Collective Action*. Cambridge: Harvard University Press.

Orfield, Gary. 1975. *Congressional Power: Congress and Social Change*. New York: Harcourt Brace Jovanovich.

Orren, Karen. 1974. *Corporate Power and Social Change*. Baltimore: The Johns Hopkins University Press.

Perry, D. June 5, 1988. "Lutheran Seminarians Face 'New Inquisition.' " *The Advocate*: 37–39.

Pinard, Maurice. 1975. *The Rise of a Third Party*. Enlarged edition. Montreal: McGill and Queen's University Press.

Pomper, Gerald. 1977. *The Election of 1976*. Ed. Marlene M. Pomper. New York: David McKay Company, Inc.

Presbyterians for Lesbian/Gay Concerns. 1985. *More Light Ministry and Outreach in the Presbyterian Church (U.S.A.)*. New Brunswick, New Jersey: PLGC.

Preston, R. K. 1986. "Asylum Adjudications: Do State Department Advisory Opinions Violate Refugees' Rights and U.S. International Obligations?" *Maryland Law Review* 45: 91–140.

Prewitt, Kenneth and Stone, Alan. 1973. *The Ruling Elites*. New York: Harper & Row.

"Psychiatrists in a Shift, Declare Homosexuality No Mental Illness." *New York Times*. December 16, 1973: 1, 25.

Ramsey, Paul. 1961. *War and the Christian Conscience: How Shall Modern War Be Conducted Justly?* Durham, North Carolina: Duke University Press.

Reichley, James. 1985. *Religion in American Public Life.* Washington, D.C.: The Brookings Institute.

Reichley, James. 1986. "Religion and the Future of American Politics." *Political Science Quarterly* 101:1: 26.

Resolutions on Lesbians, Gay Men, and Bisexuals. n.d. Prepared by the OLGC, UUA, Boston.

Robertson, D. B., ed. 1976. *Love and Justice: Selections From the Shorter Writings of Reinhold Niebuhr.* Gloucester, Massachusetts: Peter Smith.

Rogin, Michael P. 1967. *The Intellectuals and McCarthy.* Cambridge: MIT Press.

Rossiter, Clinton, ed. 1961. *The Federalist Papers.* New York: Mentor.

Salisbury, Robert H. February 1969. "An Exchange Theory of Interest Groups." *Midwest Journal of Political Science* 13: 1–32.

Schattschneider, E. E. 1935. *Politics, Pressures, and the Tariff.* Englewood Cliffs, New Jersey: Prentice-Hall.

Schattschneider, E. E. 1942. *Party Government.* New York: Farrar & Rinehart.

Schattschneider, E. E. 1960. *The Semisovereign People.* New York: Holt, Rinehart & Winston.

Sider, Ronald J. ed. 1974. *The Chicago Declaration.* Carol Stream, Illinois: Creation House.

Sider, Ronald J. 1987. *Completely Pro-Life.* Downers Grove, Illinois: InterVarsity Press.

Sider, Ronald J. September 1988. "Called to Be Servant Advocates." *ESA Advocate*: 6.

Sider, Ronald J. April 1989. "Up in Arms About Gun Control." *ESA Advocate*: 2.

Sobrino, J. June 1987. "Theological Analysis of the Sanctuary Movement." *Basta*: 19–24.

Thompson, Michael, Ellis, Richard, Wildavsky, Aaron. 1989. "Cultural Theory: Foundations of Socio-Cultural Viability." Manuscript for NEH Summer Seminar, University of California, Berkeley.

Truman, David B. 1971. *The Governmental Process.* 2nd ed. New York: Alfred A. Knopf.

Tuchman, Barbara W. April 18, 1982. "The Alternative to Arms Control." *New York Times Magazine*: 44–45, 92–95, 98–100.

Universal Fellowship Today. 1987. Los Angeles: Universal Fellowship Press.

Van Kirk, Walter. 1934. *Religion Renounces War*. Chicago: Willett, Clark and Co.

Van Ness, Daniel W. September 1988. "Crime and Its Punishment: Reforming the Judicial System." *ESA Advocate*: 3A.

Viguerie, Richard A. 1981. *The New Right: We're Ready to Lead*, revised ed. Falls Church, Virginia: The Viguerie Company.

Wald, Kenneth D. 1987. *Religion and Politics in the United States*. New York: St. Martin's Press.

Wald, K. D., Owen, D. E., and Hill, S. S. 1988. "Churches as Political Communities." *American Political Science Review* 82: 531–548.

Webber, Robert E. 1981. *The Moral Majority: Right or Wrong?* Westchester, Illinois: Cornerstone Books.

Weidenbaum, Murray L. 1975. *Government-Mandated Price Increases*. Washington, D.C.: American Enterprise Institute.

Weigel, George. 1987a. *Peace and Freedom: Christian Faith, Democracy and the Problem of War*. Washington, D.C.: The Institute on Religion and Democracy.

Weigel, George. 1987b. *Tranquillitas Ordinis: The Present Failure and Future Promise of American Catholic Thought on War and Peace*. New York: Oxford University Press.

Weinstein, James. 1968. *The Corporate Ideal and the Liberal State, 1900–1918*. Boston: Beacon Press.

Wheatley, R. 1985. *Where Love Is*. Boston: UUA.

Wiebe, Robert H. 1967. *The Search for Order*. New York: Hill & Wang.

Wildavsky, Aaron. March 1987. "Choosing Preferences by Constructing Institutions: A Cultural Theory of Preference Formation." *American Political Science Review* 81: 7.

Wildavsky, Aaron. April 1988. "Resolved, That Individualism and Egalitarianism Be Made Compatible in America: Political Cultural Roots of Exceptionalism." Paper prepared for conference on "American Exceptionalism" at Nuffield College, Oxford.

Wildavsky, Aaron. 1989. "A Cultural Theory of Leadership." In *Leadership and Politics*, ed. Bryan D. Jones. Lawrence: University Press of Kansas.

Willoughby, William. 1981. *Does America Need The Moral Majority?*
Plainfield, New Jersey: New Haven Books, a division of Logos
International.

Wilson, James Q. ed. 1980. *The Politics of Regulation.* New York:
Basic Books.

Wolfinger, Raymond E., Shapiro, Martin, and Greenstein, Fred I. eds.
1980. *Dynamics of American Politics*, 2nd Ed. Englewood
Cliffs, New Jersey: Prentice-Hall.

Wood, James E., Jr. Autumn 1980. "Religious Fundamentalism and
the New Right." *Journal of Church And State* 22: 416.

Yarnold, Barbara M. 1990. *Refugees Without Refuge: Formation and
Failed Implementation of U.S. Asylum Policy in the 1980s.*
Lanham, Maryland: University Press of America.

Yarnold, Barbara M. n.d. "The Refugee Act of 1980 and the De-
Politicization of Refugee/Asylum Admissions: An Example of
Failed Policy Implementation." *American Politics Quarterly.*

Young, Perry D. 1982. *God's Bullies.* New York: Holt, Rinehart and
Winston.

Index

Services of Union, 78
sexual activity: and the death
    penalty, 72; and equality, 111;
    and religious dogma, 72
sexual orientation, and discrimi-
    nation, 83
sexual pluralism, 77, and reli-
    gion, 77
sit-ins, 14–15, 28, 39; and abor-
    tion clinics, 28; gay and les-
    bian, 85
Smith, Al, 105
Sobrino, Jon, 31
social conservatism, 103
social gospel movement, 66, 104
social justice and gay and lesbian
    rights, 88
social movements, 33; black civil
    rights, 10–11, 14; bureaucra-
    tization of, 10; characteristics
    of, 11; conservative activism,
    10; contributory factors to
    success or failure, 10–11;
    defined, 10–11; environmen-
    talism, 10–11, 15; impacts on
    social policy, 13–14; inter-
    mediary groups, 14; middle
    class, 13–14; and moral law,
    30; and natural law, 30; and
    oligarchy, 15–16; origins of,
    30; the peace movement, 10,
    20, 29, 47, 55–58, 61, 64,
    67, 70; political dynamics of,
    14; and positive law, 21, 24;
    progressivism, 13; and public
    policy, 35–40; and special
    interests, 37; survivability, 37;
    tactics and behavior, 10, 20;
    tax revolt, 10, 20; types of,

10–12, 24; women's move-
    ment, 10–11, 13, 15, 20, 88
social reform and theological
    conservatives, 93
Society of Friends, 51; Affirm-
    ative Action Statement, 77;
    Celebration of Commitment,
    78; and employment of gays,
    77; Friends Committee for
    Lesbian and Gay Concerns, 75;
    members, 74–75
sodomy laws, 72–73
Southern Christian Leadership
    Conference, 14
special interests: control of gov-
    ernment by, 12; crusading
    against, 11; groups, 11–12
Stonewall Riots of June 1969, 73

tariffs, reduction of, 56
Tax Revolt of 1977–80, 10–20
televangelists, 94
Thomas Road Baptist Church,
    94, 105, 108
Thompson, Michael, 92, 95–96
Torah, 31
Tory armaments, 61
Toward a Quaker View of Sex,
    75
trade policy, changes in, 57
traditional pacifism, 50–51, 57,
    66–68
traditional peace churches, 51, 53
treaties, limitations of, 62–63
Treaty of Locarno, 58
Treaty of Versailles, 53, 59
treaty violations, 53, 61
Tucson Ecumenical Council, 32
Tucson Trial, 34, 39

ABOUT THE CONTRIBUTORS

STEVEN H. HAEBERLE is Associate Professor of the Department of Political Science and Public Affairs at the University of Alabama at Birmingham.

MEL HAILEY is Chairman of the Department of Political Science at Abilene Christian University.

WILLIAM R. MARTY is Professor of the Department of Political Science at Memphis State University.

ANDREW S. McFARLAND is Associate Professor of the Department of Political Science at the University of Illinois, at Chicago.

BARBARA M. YARNOLD is Assistant Professor in the Department of Public Administration at Florida International University.